Houghton
Mifflin
Harcourt

TEXAS SCIENCE fusion

fusion [FYOO • zhuhn] a combination of two or more things that releases energy

This Write-In Student Edition belongs to

_____

Teacher/Room

_____

Consulting Authors

Michael A. DiSpezio
Global Educator
North Falmouth, Massachusetts

Marjorie Frank
Science Writer and Content-Area Reading Specialist
Brooklyn, New York

Michael Heithaus
Executive Director, School of Environment, Arts, and Society
Associate Professor, Department of Biological Sciences
Florida International University
North Miami, Florida

Donna Ogle
Professor of Reading and Language
National-Louis University
Chicago, Illinois

Front Cover: *turtle* ©Westend61 GmbH/Alamy; *bubbles* ©Andrew Holt/Alamy; *guitar* ©Brand Z/Alamy; *giraffe* ©Nicholas Eveleigh/Stockbyte/Getty Images; *observatory* ©Robert Llewellyn/Workbook Stock/Getty Images; *wind turbine* ©Comstock/Getty Images.

Back Cover: *prism* ©Larry Lilac/Alamy; *clownfish* ©Georgette Douwma/Photographer's Choice/Getty Images; *galaxy* ©Stocktrek/Corbis; *fern* ©Mauro Fermariello/Photo Researchers, Inc.

Printed in the U.S.A.

ISBN 978-0-544-02547-9

11 12 0928 21 20 19

4500742814 BCDEFG

Program Advisors

Paul D. Asimow
Professor of Geology and Geochemistry
California Institute of Technology
Pasadena, California

Bobby Jeanpierre
*Associate Professor of Science
    Education*
University of Central Florida
Orlando, Florida

Gerald H. Krockover
*Professor Emeritus of Earth,
    Atmospheric, and Planetary
    Science Education*
Purdue University
West Lafayette, Indiana

Rose Pringle
*Associate Professor
    School of Teaching and Learning*
College of Education
University of Florida
Gainesville, Florida

Carolyn Staudt
Curriculum Designer for Technology
KidSolve, Inc.
The Concord Consortium
Concord, Massachusetts

Larry Stookey
Science Department
Antigo High School
Antigo, Wisconsin

Carol J. Valenta
*Associate Director of the Museum and
    Senior Vice President*
Saint Louis Science Center
St. Louis, Missouri

Barry A. Van Deman
President and CEO
Museum of Life and Science
Durham, North Carolina

Texas Reviewers

Max Ceballos
District Science Specialist
Edinburg, Texas

Tamara L. Cryar
Cook Elementary
Austin, Texas

Heather Domjan
University of Houston
Houston, Texas

Ashley D. Golden
Washington Elementary
Big Spring, Texas

Linda Churchwell Halliman
Cornelius Elementary School
Houston, Texas

Ellen Lyon
Hays Consolidated ISD
Kyle, Texas

Stephanie McNeil
Bastian Elementary
Houston, Texas

Sue Mendoza
District Science Coach
El Paso ISD
El Paso, Texas

Christine L. Morgan
Emerson Elementary
Midland, Texas

Genaro Ovalle III
Elementary Science Dean
Laredo ISD
Laredo, Texas

Hilda Quintanar
Science Coach
El Paso ISD
El Paso, Texas

Power up with Texas Science Fusion!

Grade 2

Your program fuses...

e-Learning & Virtual Labs

Labs & Explorations

Write-In Student Edition

...to generate new energy for today's science learner— you.

Write-In Student Edition

Be an active reader and make this book your own!

Food for Th

Food is an important need for ani
umans. Food helps animals and huma
d change. Some animals eat plants. Some
r animals. Other animals and humans may
th plants and animals.

Write your ideas, answer questions, make notes, and record activity results right on these pages.

▶ Dr   a food you like   at.

Learn science concepts and skills by interacting with every page.

e-Learning & Virtual Labs

Digital lessons and virtual labs provide e-learning options for every lesson of *Science Fusion*.

On your own or with a group, explore science concepts in a digital world.

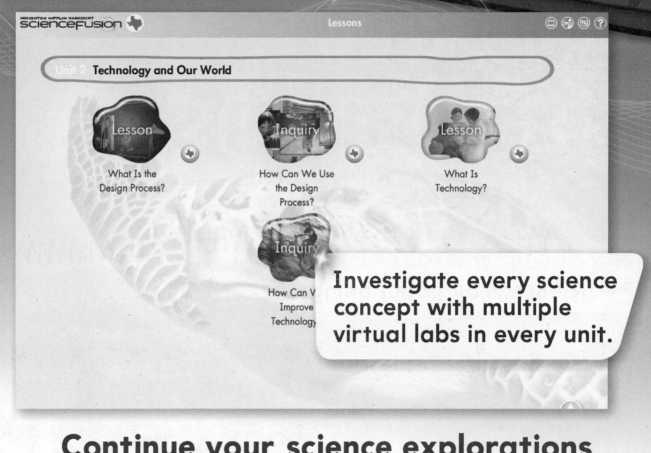

Unit 2 Technology and Our World

Lesson
What Is the Design Process?

Inquiry
How Can We Use the Design Process?

Lesson
What Is Technology?

Inquiry
How Can We Improve Technology?

Investigate every science concept with multiple virtual labs in every unit.

Continue your science explorations with these online tools:

→ ScienceSaurus   → People in Science

→ NSTA Scilinks   → Media Gallery

→ Video-based Projects   → Vocabulary Cards

→ Science Readers for Texas with complete AUDIO!

What Can We Learn About Matter?

What Can We Learn About Matter?

Making Coins

Labs & Explorations

Science is all about doing.

Exciting investigations for every lesson.

Ask questions and test your ideas.

Draw conclusions and share what you learn.

How Does the Sun Warm Our Homes?

How does solar energy warm our homes? Make a model to find out.

Materials

cardboard box   tape

scissors   2 thermometers

plastic wrap

1 Use the box and the plastic wrap to make a model house. **Caution!** Be careful when using scissors.

2 Tape one thermometer into a window of the house. Record the temperatures on both thermometers.

3 Put the house in a sunny spot. Lay the other thermometer next to the house. Wait 1 hour. Record both temperatures again. Compare the numbers.

Get Real!

Look at the engineers at work! **Engineers** solve problems by using math and science. The answers they find help people.

Engineers work in many areas. Some engineers design cars. Some make robots. Others find ways to make the world cleaner or safer.

Active Reading

Find the sentence that tells the meaning of **engineers**. Draw a line under that sentence.

The Design Process

How do engineers solve a problem? They use a design process. A **design process** is a set of steps that engineers follow to solve problems.

This engineer checks on a building project.

A civil engi...
bridges an...

44

45

S.T.E.M.
Engineering and Technology

How It's Made
Cotton Shirt

A cotton shirt is made from cotton plants. It takes many steps to make cotton into a shirt.

Raw cotton is picked and cleaned.

The cotton is spun into thread. The thread is woven into fabric.

...correct
...g a cotton

...elp make cotton into a shirt?

...ut building safety. Complete
...ldings on the ... Flipchart.

By asking questions, testing your ideas, organizing and analyzing data, drawing conclusions, and sharing what you learn...

You are the scientist!

Texas Essential Knowledge and Skills

Dear Students and Family Members,

The *ScienceFusion* Student Edition, Inquiry Flipchart, and Digital Curriculum provide a full year of interactive experiences built around the Texas Essential Knowledge and Skills for Science. As you read, experiment, and interact with print and digital content, you will be learning what you need to know for this school year. The Texas Essential Knowledge and Skills are listed here for you. You will also see them referenced throughout this book. Look for them on the opening pages of each unit and lesson.

Have a great school year!

Sincerely,
The HMH *ScienceFusion* Team

Look in each unit to find the picture.

Check it out:
Unit 5 This picture is found on page ____.

TEKS 2.1

Scientific investigation and reasoning.
The student conducts classroom and outdoor investigations following home and school safety procedures. The student is expected to:

A identify and demonstrate safe practices as described in the Texas Safety Standards during classroom and outdoor investigations, including wearing safety goggles, washing hands, and using materials appropriately;

B describe the importance of safe practices; and

C identify and demonstrate how to use, conserve, and dispose of natural resources and materials such as conserving water and reuse or recycling of paper, plastic, and metal.

Answer Key: page 211

Check it out:
Unit 1 This picture is found on page ____.

Check it out:
Unit 2 This picture is found on page ____.

Check it out:
Unit 1 This picture is found on page ____.

TEKS 2.2

Scientific investigation and reasoning.
The student develops abilities necessary to do scientific inquiry in classroom and outdoor investigations. The student is expected to:

A ask questions about organisms, objects, and events during observations and investigations;

B plan and conduct descriptive investigations such as how organisms grow;

C collect data from observations using simple equipment such as hand lenses, primary balances, thermometers, and non-standard measurement tools;

D record and organize data using pictures, numbers, and words;

E communicate observations and justify explanations using student-generated data from simple descriptive investigations; and

F compare results of investigations with what students and scientists know about the world.

TEKS 2.3

Scientific investigation and reasoning.
The student knows that information and critical thinking, scientific problem solving, and the contributions of scientists are used in making decisions. The student is expected to:

A identify and explain a problem in his/her own words and propose a task and solution for the problem such as lack of water in a habitat;

B make predictions based on observable patterns; and

C identify what a scientist is and explore what different scientists do.

TEKS 2.4

Science investigation and reasoning.
The student uses age-appropriate tools and models to investigate the natural world. The student is expected to:

A collect, record, and compare information using tools, including computers, hand lenses, rulers, primary balances, plastic beakers, magnets, collecting nets, notebooks, and safety goggles; timing devices, including clocks and stopwatches; weather instruments such as thermometers, wind vanes, and rain gauges; and materials to support observations of habitats of organisms such as terrariums and aquariums; and

B measure and compare organisms and objects using non-standard units that approximate metric units.

Check it out:
Unit 3 This picture is found on page _____.

Check it out:
Unit 4 This picture is found on page _____.

Check it out:
Unit 5 This picture is found on page _____.

TEKS 2.5

Matter and energy. The student knows that matter has physical properties and those properties determine how it is described, classified, changed, and used. The student is expected to:

A classify matter by physical properties, including shape, relative mass, relative temperature, texture, flexibility, and whether material is a solid or liquid;

B compare changes in materials caused by heating and cooling;

C demonstrate that things can be done to materials to change their physical properties such as cutting, folding, sanding, and melting; and

D combine materials that when put together can do things that they cannot do by themselves such as building a tower or a bridge and justify the selection of those materials based on their physical properties.

TEKS 2.6

Force, motion, and energy. The student knows that forces cause change and energy exists in many forms. The student is expected to:

A investigate the effects on an object by increasing or decreasing amounts of light, heat, and sound energy such as how the color of an object appears different in dimmer light or how heat melts butter;

B observe and identify how magnets are used in everyday life;

C trace the changes in the position of an object over time such as a cup rolling on the floor and a car rolling down a ramp; and

D compare patterns of movement of objects such as sliding, rolling, and spinning.

TEKS 2.7

Earth and space. The student knows that the natural world includes earth materials. The student is expected to:

A observe and describe rocks by size, texture, and color;

B identify and compare the properties of natural sources of freshwater and saltwater; and

C distinguish between natural and manmade resources.

Answer Key: page 102, page 158, page 168

Check it out:
Unit 6 This picture is found on page _____.

Check it out:
Unit 8 This picture is found on page _____.

Check it out:
Unit 9 This picture is found on page _____.

TEKS 2.8

Earth and space. The student knows that there are recognizable patterns in the natural world and among objects in the sky. The student is expected to:

A measure, record, and graph weather information, including temperature, wind conditions, precipitation, and cloud coverage, in order to identify patterns in the data;

B identify the importance of weather and seasonal information to make choices in clothing, activities, and transportation;

C explore the processes in the water cycle, including evaporation, condensation, and precipitation, as connected to weather conditions; and

D observe, describe, and record patterns of objects in the sky, including the appearance of the Moon.

TEKS 2.9

Organisms and environments. The student knows that living organisms have basic needs that must be met for them to survive within their environment. The student is expected to:

A identify the basic needs of plants and animals;

B identify factors in the environment, including temperature and precipitation, that affect growth and behavior such as migration, hibernation, and dormancy of living things; and

C compare and give examples of the ways living organisms depend on each other and on their environments such as food chains within a garden, park, beach, lake, and wooded area.

TEKS 2.10

Organisms and environments. The student knows that organisms resemble their parents and have structures and processes that help them survive within their environments. The student is expected to:

A observe, record, and compare how the physical characteristics and behaviors of animals help them meet their basic needs such as fins help fish move and balance in the water;

B observe, record, and compare how the physical characteristics of plants help them meet their basic needs such as stems carry water throughout the plant; and

C investigate and record some of the unique stages that insects undergo during their life cycle.

Answer Key: page 253, page 302, page 346

Contents

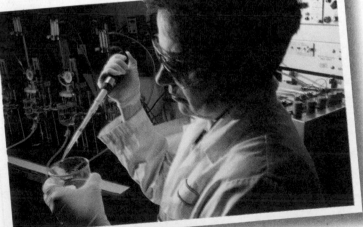

© Houghton Mifflin Harcourt Publishing Company   (b) ©Geostock/Getty Images

EARTH SCIENCE

Safety in Science

Indoors Doing science is fun. But a science lab can be dangerous. Know the safety rules and listen to your teacher.

Follow these indoor science safety rules.

1 **Think ahead.** Study the steps. Follow them.

2 **Be neat.** Wipe up spills right away. Keep hair and clothing out of the way.

3 **Oops!** Tell your teacher if you spill or break something or get hurt.

4 **Watch your eyes.** Wear safety goggles when the teacher tells you.

5 **Ouch!** Do not touch sharp things.

6 **Yuck!** Do not eat or drink things unless the teacher tells you.

7 **Don't get shocked.** Do not touch electric outlets.

8 **Keep it clean.** Clean up afterward. Wash your hands.

Outdoors Lots of science happens outdoors. Exploring the wilderness or your backyard is fun! But you need to be careful.

Follow these outdoor science safety rules.

1. **Think ahead.** Study the steps. Follow them.

2. **Dress right.** Wear clothes and shoes that are right for outdoors.

3. **Cover up.** Follow sun safety rules.

4. **Oops!** Tell your teacher if you break something or get hurt.

5. **Watch your eyes.** Tell your teacher right away if anything gets in your eyes. Wear goggles when your teacher tells you.

6. **Yuck!** Never taste anything outdoors unless the teacher tells you.

7. **Stay together.** Stay on marked trails.

8. **Do not act wild.** No horseplay or pranks.

9. **Always walk.** No running!

10. **Clean up the area.** Throw away litter as your teacher tells you.

11. **Clean up.** Wash your hands with soap and water when you're done.

Work Like a Scientist

Thomas Edison's lab

Big Idea

Scientists ask questions about the world around them. They find answers by investigating through many methods.

TEKS 2.2A, 2.2B, 2.2D, 2.2E, 2.3A, 2.3B, 2.3C, 2.4A, 2.4B

I Wonder Why

Scientists use tools to find out about things. Why?
Turn the page to find out.

Here's Why Tools help scientists learn more than they could with just their senses.

In this unit, you will explore this Big Idea, the Essential Questions, and the Investigations on the Inquiry Flipchart.

Levels of Inquiry Key ■ DIRECTED ■ GUIDED ■ INDEPENDENT

Track Your Progress

Big Idea Scientists ask questions about the world around them. They find answers by investigating through many methods.

Essential Questions

Science Notebook

Before you begin each lesson, be sure to write your thoughts about the Essential Question.

TEKS **2.2A** ask questions about organisms, objects, and events during observations and investigations **2.2D** record and organize data using pictures, numbers, and words

Lesson **1**

Essential Question

How Do We Use Inquiry Skills?

Engage Your Brain!

Find the answer in this lesson.

You tell how these flowers are alike and different.

You are

_____ them.

Active Reading

Lesson Vocabulary

1 Preview the lesson.

2 Write the vocabulary term here.

_____

Use Inquiry Skills

Inquiry skills help people find out information. Inquiry skills help people plan and do tests.

Danny and Sophie use inquiry skills to do a task for school. They want to find out what they can observe in a backyard. Observe means to use your five senses to learn about things.

Active Reading

Find the sentence that tells the meaning of **observe**. Draw a line under the sentence.

> What can we observe in my backyard?

4

The children ask a question—What can we observe in a backyard? They plan an investigation to find out what they want to know. They also predict, or make a good guess, about what they will observe.

▶ This page names three inquiry skills. Circle the name for one of the skills.

Explore the Backyard

Danny and Sophie head out to the backyard to begin their task. Danny measures, or finds the length and the height of, the birdhouse. He measures it with a ruler.

Active Reading

Find the sentence that explains what it means to **measure**. Draw a line under the sentence.

They use inquiry skills to learn more about the backyard.

Sophie compares leaves. She observes how they are alike and how they are different. She may also classify, or sort, leaves in the backyard by the way they are alike.

▶ Look at Sophie's leaves. Organize them by size from smallest to largest.

_____   _____   _____

Model and Infer

Now Danny and Sophie draw a map of the backyard. They are making a model to show what something is like. You could also make a model to show how something works.

My Backyard

birch tree

rose bush

maple tree

bird bath

bird house

Active Reading

Find the sentences that explain what it means to **make a model**. Draw a line under the sentences.

Danny and Sophie use one more inquiry skill. They infer. They use what they know to answer a question—Are there any living things in the backyard? They can infer that the backyard is home to many plants and animals.

▶ What is another question Danny and Sophie might ask about the living things in the backyard? Write a question.

_____

_____

Sum It Up!

1 Complete It!

Fill in the blank.

How are measuring, observing, and predicting alike?

They are all

_____ .

2 Circle It!

Circle the skill name to match the meaning.

Which one means to choose steps you will do to learn something?

infer

plan an investigation

classify

3 Draw and Write It!

Observe something outside. Then draw and write to record your observations.

_____

_____

Name _____

Word Play

Read each clue below. Then unscramble the letters to write the correct answer.

observe	compare	measure	infer

1 to find the size or amount of something

s e m a r e u _____

2 to use your senses to learn about something

b o s r e e v _____

3 to observe how things are alike and different

p o c r a m e _____

4 to use what you know to answer a question

f n i r e _____

Match each inquiry skill to its meaning.

to make a good guess about what will happen	plan an investigation
to sort things by how they are alike	classify
to show what something is like or how it works	predict
to follow steps to answer a question	make a model

Take It Home!

Family Members: Work with your child to measure two objects in your home. Have your child compare the two objects and tell which is larger.

TEKS **2.4A** collect, record, and compare information using tools, including...hand lenses, rulers, primary balances **2.4B** measure and compare organisms and objects using non-standard units that approximate metric units

Essential Question

What Are Science Tools?

Engage Your Brain!

Find the answer to the question in the lesson.

What does a thermometer measure?

_____

Active Reading

Lesson Vocabulary

1 Preview the lesson.

2 Write the 2 vocabulary terms here.

_____ _____

Units to Know

Some tools have two units of measurement on them. Before you start using tools, it is good to know how to read their measurements!

Take a look at the ruler below. You can use both sides of the ruler to measure objects. You can use one side of the ruler to measure in centimeters. You can use the other side of the ruler to measure in inches.

Active Reading

A detail is a fact about a main idea. Draw one line under a detail. Draw an arrow to the main idea it tells about.

inches

Sometimes tools are not around when we need them. We can use everyday objects to measure things. For example, you could use paper clips to measure the width of your desk.

Do the Math!
Measure Width

Measure the width of the top of your desk in paper clips.

_____ paper clips

How many centimeters do you think the paper clips equal? Measure with a ruler.

_____ centimeters

centimeters

Top Tools

You use tools every day. Tools are things that help you do a job. **Science tools** are tools you use to find out information.

A hand lens is one science tool. It helps you observe more details than with your eyes alone.

▶ What can you see through this hand lens? Circle it.

A hand lens makes things look larger.

Measuring Tools

You use some tools for measuring things. A **thermometer** is a tool you use to measure temperature. You use a measuring cup to measure amounts of liquids.

Active Reading

The main idea is the most important idea about something. Draw a line under the main idea on this page.

A thermometer measures in units called degrees Celsius and degrees Fahrenheit.

A measuring cup measures liquids in units called milliliters, cups, and ounces.

Measure More!

You use a tool called a scale to measure weight. You can use a balance to measure mass.

This scale measures weight in units called pounds and ounces.

▶ Name two things you can weigh on a scale.

_____

_____

This balance measures mass in units called grams and kilograms.

You use a ruler and a tape measure to measure distance as well as length, width, and height. Both tools measure in units called inches or centimeters.

▶ Circle the object the ruler is measuring.

A ruler measures objects with straight lines.

A tape measure can measure around an object.

Sum It Up!

1 Answer It!

Write the answer to this question.

You want to measure how much water fits into a pail. What tool could you use?

_____

2 Circle It!

Circle the answer.

A measuring cup can measure in cups or in _____.

inches

milliliters

grams

3 Mark It!

Mark an X on the tool that does _not_ measure.

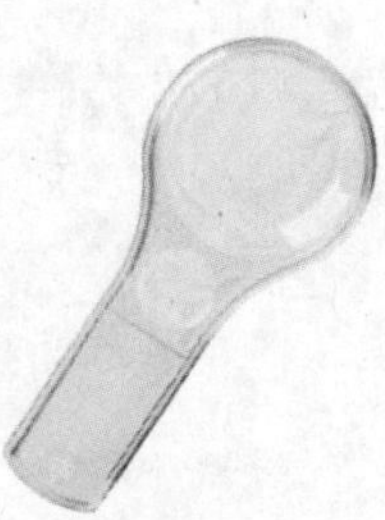

20

Brain Check

Name_____

Word Play

Match the name of each tool to its picture.

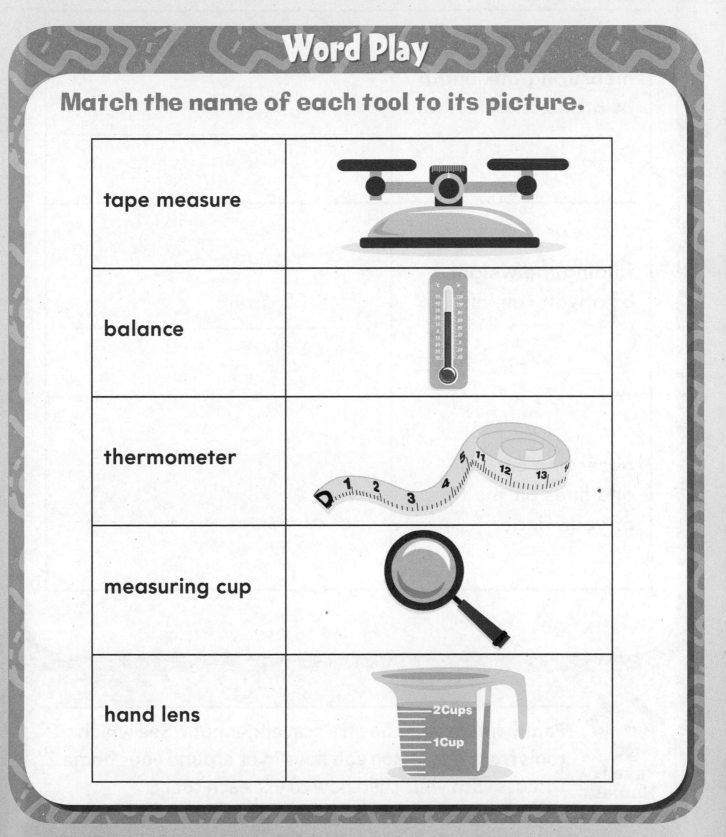

tape measure	
balance	
thermometer	
measuring cup	
hand lens	

Apply Concepts

Name the tool you could use for each job.

measuring the length of a book	_____
finding the weight of a watermelon	_____
observing curves and lines on the tip of your finger	_____

Take It Home!

Family Members: Go on a scavenger hunt. See which tools from this lesson you have in or around your home. Discuss with your child how to use each tool.

TEKS **2.3C** identify what a scientist is and explore what different scientists do **2.4A** collect, record, and compare information using tools, including...weather instruments such as thermometers

People in Science

1

In 1742, Celsius invented the Celsius scale to measure temperature.

2

The temperature at which water freezes on the Celsius scale is 0°.

4

Things to Know About

Anders Celsius

3

The temperature at which water boils on the Celsius scale is 100°.

4

Celsius was an astronomer, or a person who studies the stars and other things in space.

© Houghton Mifflin Harcourt Publishing Company (bkgd) ©Photomorgana/Corbis; (tc) ©Mary Evans Picture Library/Alamy

Celsius Match Up

► Read and compare each thermometer.
Write the number that matches the correct
temperature in each picture.

1

2

3

► How does a temperature scale help you tell
about the weather?

_____

_____

TEKS **2.2A** ask questions about organisms, objects, and events during observations and investigations **2.2B** plan and conduct descriptive investigations such as how organisms grow **2.2C** collect data from observations using simple equipment such as hand lenses, primary balances, thermometers, and non-standard measurement tools **2.2E** communicate observations and justify explanations using student-generated data from simple descriptive investigations **2.4A** collect, record, and compare information using tools, including...hand lenses, rulers

Name _____

Essential Question

What Tools Can We Use?

Set a Purpose

Write what you want to find out.

_____

_____

Think About the Procedure

1 Which science tool did you choose? What does it do?

_____

_____

2 How will the tool help you collect information about the object?

_____

_____

Record Your Data

Use your data to communicate your observations.

My Object _____	
My Tool _____	
What I Learned Without the Tool	What I Learned With the Tool

Draw Conclusions

How can a science tool help you learn more about an object?

_____

_____

_____

Ask More Questions

Ask questions about the tools used in your investigation. What other questions can you ask about how science tools are used?

_____

_____

_____

TEKS **2.3B** make predictions based on observable patterns **2.3C** identify what a scientist is and explore what different scientists do **2.4A** collect, record, and compare information using tools, including...rulers

Essential Question

How Do Scientists Think?

Find the answer in the lesson.

When scientists

_____

they follow steps and use tools to answer a question.

Active Reading

Lesson Vocabulary

1 Preview the lesson.

2 Write the 4 vocabulary terms here.

_____ _____

_____ _____

Let's Observe It!

A scientist is someone who explores the world around them. Scientists investigate. To **investigate** you plan and do a test to answer a question or solve a problem. Scientists use inquiry skills and science tools to help them.

Many scientists follow a sequence, or order of events, when they investigate. Here's one possible sequence. First, scientists may observe and ask a question.

Active Reading

Clue words can help you find the order of things. **First** is a clue word. Circle this clue word in the paragraph above.

Does food coloring spread faster in cold water or warm water?

cold

Now, scientists can make a hypothesis. A **hypothesis** is a statement that can be tested. Then scientists plan a fair test. The scientists list the materials they will need and the steps they will take to do their test.

▶ Identify what a scientist is. Write your answer.

_____

_____

_____

Food coloring spreads faster in warm water.

food coloring

warm

29

Let's Test It!

Next, the scientists are ready to do their test. They follow their plan and record what they observe.

Active Reading

Clue words can help you find the order of things. **Next** is a clue word. Circle this clue word in the paragraph above.

These children test whether food coloring spreads faster in cold water or warm water.

cold

warm

Cold

After the test, scientists draw conclusions. To **draw conclusions**, you use the information you have gathered to decide if your results support the hypothesis. Finally, they **communicate**, or write and draw, what they learned.

▶ **How does the temperature of water affect how fast the food coloring spreads? Draw a conclusion.**

_____

_____

_____

▶ **What else could a scientist test with water and food coloring?**

_____

_____

_____

warm

Let's Check Again!

Scientists do the same test a few times. They need to make sure that they get similar results every time. In this investigation, the food coloring should spread faster in warm water every time.

Our Food Colorir

| cold | warm | cold | warm |

Monday   Wednesday

► Look at the cups. Make a prediction about what the **warm** cup for Wednesday should look like. Color the cup to show your prediction.

Choose an object. Use a ruler to measure the object's length. Measure it three times. Record.

Length of _____	
Measure 1	
Measure 2	
Measure 3	

1. How do your numbers compare?

_____

_____

2. Why do you think so?

_____

_____

_____

Sum It Up!

① Order It!

Number the steps from 1 to 4 to tell a way scientists investigate.

_____ Observe and ask a question.

_____ Do the test and record what happens.

_____ Draw conclusions and communicate.

_____ Make a hypothesis and plan a fair test.

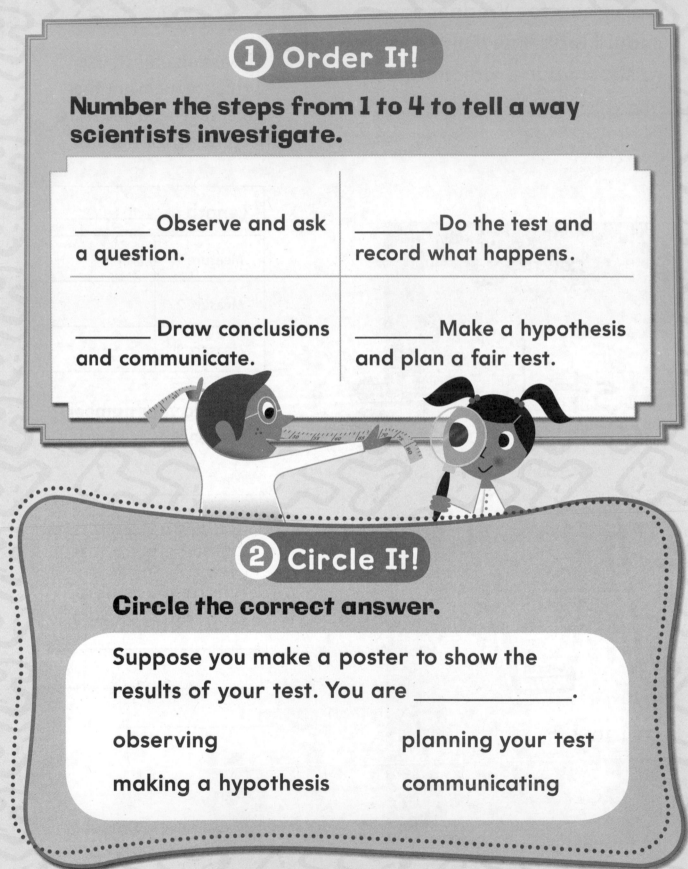

② Circle It!

Circle the correct answer.

Suppose you make a poster to show the results of your test. You are _____.

observing   planning your test

making a hypothesis   communicating

Name _____

Word Play

Circle the word to complete each sentence.

1 You use inquiry skills and science tools to do a test to answer a question. You _____.

communicate   investigate

2 You take the first step to do an investigation. You _____.

draw conclusions   observe

3 You make a statement that you can test. You make a _____.

hypothesis   conclusion

4 You use information you gathered to decide if your results support the hypothesis. You _____.

draw conclusions   observe

5 You draw or write to tell about the results of a test. You _____.

communicate   ask a question

Apply Concepts

These steps show a test some children did.
Label each box with a step from this lesson.

The children look at an ice cube. They ask—
Will it melt in the sun?

Observe and _____.

They form a statement that the ice cube will melt
in the sun.

_____.

They follow their plan. The ice cube melts! They
decide that the sun's heat caused the ice to melt.

Test and _____.

The children write and draw to tell the results
of their test.

_____.

Take It Home!

Family Members: Work with your child to plan an
investigation. Use the steps from this lesson.

TEKS **2.2A** ask questions about organisms, objects, and events during observations and investigations **2.2B** plan and conduct descriptive investigations such as how organisms grow **2.2D** record and organize data using pictures, numbers, and words **2.3A** identify and explain a problem in his/her own words and propose a task and solution for the problem such as lack of water in a habitat

Name _____

Essential Question

How Do We Solve a Problem?

Set a Purpose

Identify and explain the problem you want to solve.

_____

_____

Think About the Procedure

1 Why do you make a list of the properties the holder must have?

_____

_____

2 Why do you design your holder before you build it?

_____

_____

Record Your Data

Record the details of your plan in this chart.

The Problem	
My Solution	
Materials I need	

Draw Conclusions

Sometimes it is helpful to make a model first before making the real thing. How can making a model help you solve a problem?

_____

_____

Ask More Questions

What other questions do you have about making models to solve problems?

_____

_____

Vocabulary Review

Use the terms in the box to complete the sentences.

> communicate
> investigate
> thermometer

TEKS 2.2E

1. When you draw or write, you
   _____.

TEKS 2.4A

2. A tool that measures temperature is a(n)
   _____.

TEKS 2.2B

3. When you plan and do a test to answer a
   question, you _____.

Science Concepts

Fill in the letter of the choice that best answers the question.

TEKS 2.2A

4. Sumeet has a book and a ruler. Which question can he answer using these objects?

   Ⓐ What is the weight of the book?

   Ⓑ What is the mass of the book?

   Ⓒ What is the length of the book?

TEKS 2.2B

5. Lea plans an investigation about plant growth. She does a test to see how much sun plants need. What should she do after her test?

   Ⓐ draw conclusions

   Ⓑ communicate what she learned

   Ⓒ make a hypothesis

TEKS 2.4A

6. Reem uses this tool to find the length of a book.

1 2 3 4 5 6 7 8 9 10 11 12
centimeters

What is she doing?

Ⓐ classifying

Ⓑ inferring

Ⓒ measuring

TEKS 2.4A

7. Jia wants to find out how the temperature in the afternoon compares to the morning temperature. What should she do?

Ⓐ Infer the afternoon temperature. Then compare it to the morning temperature.

Ⓑ Measure the afternoon temperature with a thermometer. Then compare it to the morning temperature.

Ⓒ Predict the afternoon temperature. Then compare it to the morning temperature.

TEKS 2.2C

8. Victor weighs a melon on a scale. The melon weighs 3 pounds. Ana also measures the weight of the same melon. What should Ana observe?

Ⓐ The melon weighs 2 pounds.

Ⓑ The melon weighs 3 pounds.

Ⓒ The melon weighs 4 pounds.

TEKS 2.2D

9. Carlos finishes an investigation. He draws this picture in a notebook.

Why does Carlos draw the picture?

Ⓐ to plan the investigation

Ⓑ to predict what will happen

Ⓒ to record what he observed

TEKS 2.2B

10. Troy wants to know if plants grow better in light or shade. How can he find out?

  Ⓐ He can grow two different plants in light. Then he can compare the results.

  Ⓑ He can grow two different plants in shade. Then he can compare the results.

  Ⓒ He can grow one plant in light and one plant in shade. Then he can compare the results.

TEKS 2.3C

11. How do scientists work to solve problems?

  Ⓐ They solve problems the same way each time.

  Ⓑ They always work alone.

  Ⓒ They keep looking for new ways to solve problems.

TEKS 2.4A

12. Kate wants to know whether a book or a pencil has more mass. Which tool should she use?

  Ⓐ
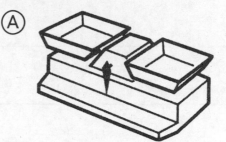

  Ⓑ
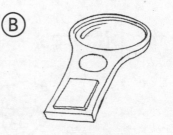

  Ⓒ

Inquiry and the Big Idea
Write the answers to these questions.

TEKS 2.2B

13. You complete an investigation about plants. Now you have another question. What should you do?

_____

_____

TEKS 2.4A

14. Look at the picture.

a. What science tool is the boy using?

_____

b. What is he doing?

_____

Technology and Our World

Big Idea

Information and critical thinking, scientific problem solving, and the contributions of scientists are used in making decisions.

Rocket Park, Houston, Texas

TEKS 2.2A, 2.2B, 2.2D, 2.2E, 2.3A, 2.3C

I Wonder How

Engineers planned designs for these rockets and this space suit. How?

Turn the page to find out.

Here's How Engineers made plans for the rockets and the space suit. The plans showed how they would be built.

In this unit, you will explore this Big Idea, the Essential Questions, and the Investigations on the Inquiry Flipchart.

Levels of Inquiry Key ■ DIRECTED ■ GUIDED ■ INDEPENDENT

Track Your Progress

Big Idea Information and critical thinking, scientific problem solving, and the contributions of scientists are used in making decisions.

Essential Questions

Now I Get the Big Idea!

Science Notebook

Before you begin each lesson, be sure to write your thoughts about the Essential Question.

TEKS 2.3A identify and explain a problem in his/her own words and propose a task and solution for the problem such as lack of water in a habitat 2.3C identify what a scientist is and explore what different scientists do

Essential Question

What Is the Design Process?

Engage Your Brain!

Find the answer to the question in the lesson.

How could you keep the dog leashes from getting tangled?

You could _____

_____.

Active Reading

Lesson Vocabulary

1 Preview the lesson.

2 Write the 2 vocabulary terms here.

_____ _____

Get Real!

Look at the engineers at work! An **engineer** is a person who solves problems by using math and science. The answers an engineer finds help people.

Engineers work in many areas. Some engineers design cars. Some make robots. Others find ways to make the world cleaner or safer.

Active Reading

Find the sentence that tells the meaning of **engineer**. Draw a line under that sentence.

A civil engineer plans bridges and roads.

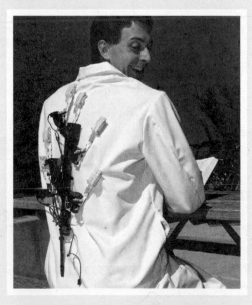

A robotics engineer designs robots.

The Design Process

How do engineers solve a problem? They use a design process. A **design process** is a set of steps that engineers follow to solve problems.

This engineer checks on a building project.

▶ Read the captions. Circle the names of three kinds of engineers.

An aerospace engineer may work on airplanes or rockets.

A Tangled Mess!

When Kate walks her dogs, their leashes always get tangled. She needs to solve this problem. How can a design process help?

1 Find a Problem

Kate's first step is to name her problem. What is wrong? What does she want to do? Then Kate brainstorms ways to solve her problem.

Active Reading

Things may happen in order. Write 1 next to what happens first. Write 2 next to what happens next.

Kate gets out her science notebook. She will keep good records. She will show how she plans and builds the solution to her problem.

Problem—
My dogs' leashes keep tangling.

Brainstorm solutions—

▶ Draw a solution for Kate's problem.

2 Plan and Build

Next, Kate chooses a solution to try. She makes a plan. She draws and labels her plan.

Kate chooses materials that are good for leashes. Look at Kate's materials. What materials would you choose?

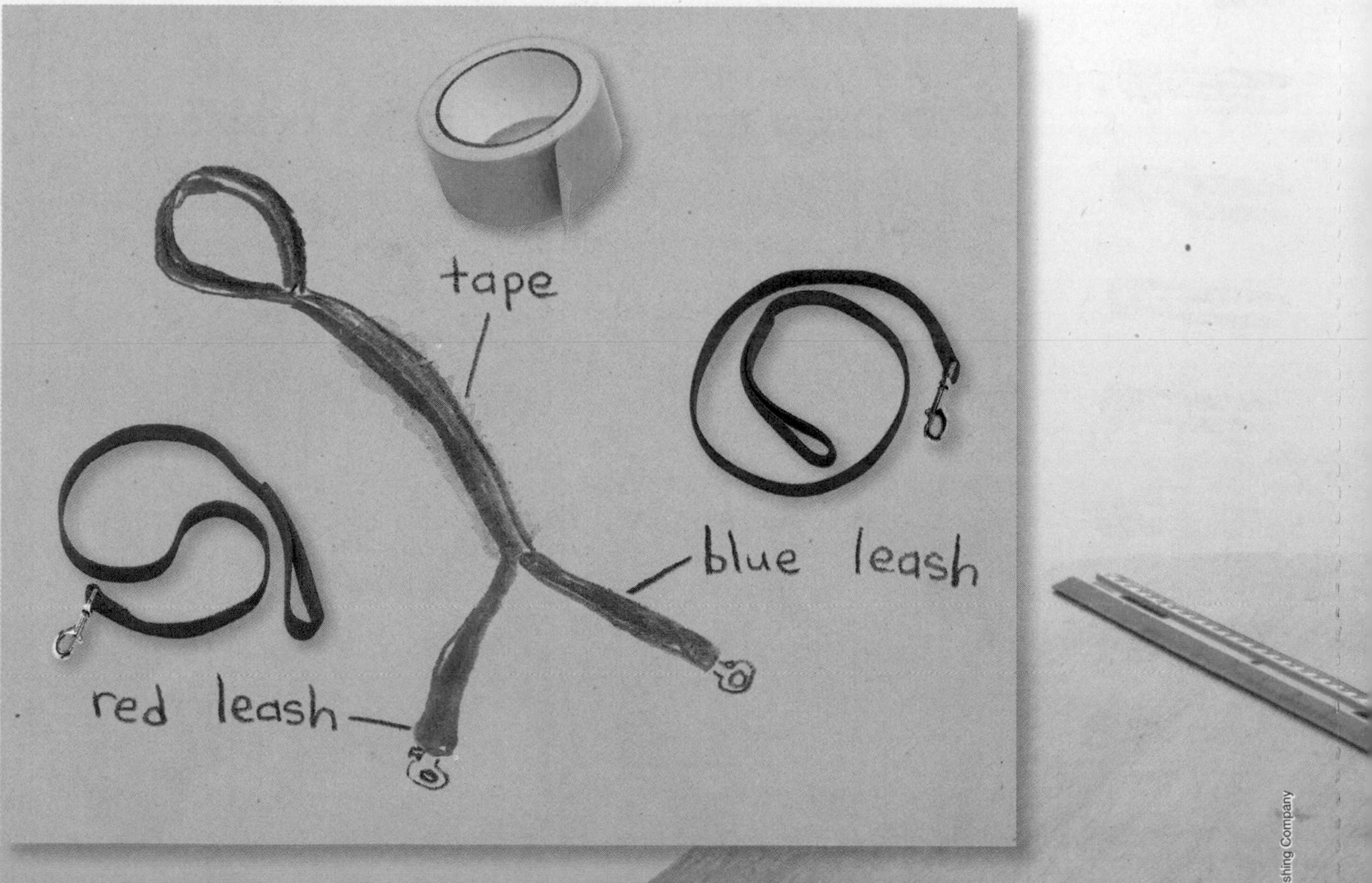

tape

red leash

blue leash

Kate follows her plan to make her new leash.
The new leash may be the solution to her problem!

▶ How does planning help Kate build her new leash?

_____

_____

3 Test and Improve

It is time for Kate to find out whether the new leash works. She tests it when she walks the dogs. Kate will know the leash works if it does not tangle.

4 Redesign

Kate thinks of ways to improve her new leash. She writes notes about how to make her design better.

5 Communicate

Kate shows the results of her test. She takes a picture of her design. She also writes about what happened during the test.

Ways to make the design better—make the leash parts or the handle longer.

My Results—
1. Red and blue parts of the new leash did not tangle.
2. My feet bumped the dogs as I walked.

▶ Circle the part of the results that tells about a problem with the leash.

Sum It Up!

① Circle It!

Circle the step of the design process shown here.

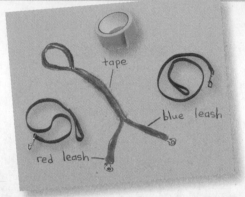

Test and Improve

Plan and Build

Find a Problem

② Write It!

Write the answer to the question.

Why is it important to keep good records?

_____

_____

_____

_____

Name _____

Word Play

Write a term for each definition.

design process	materials	solution	test

steps that engineers follow to solve a problem

__ __ __ __ __ __ __   __ __ __ __ __ __ __
   1   3 2

the answer to a problem

__ __ __ __ __ __ __ __
              4   5

how you find out whether a solution works

__ __ __ __
   6

things you use to make a design

__ __ __ __ __ __ __ __ __
    7 8

Solve the riddle. Write the numbered letters in order on the lines below.

I am a scientist who uses math and science to solve problems. Who am I?

__ __ __ __ __ __ __ __
1 2 3 4 5 6 7 8

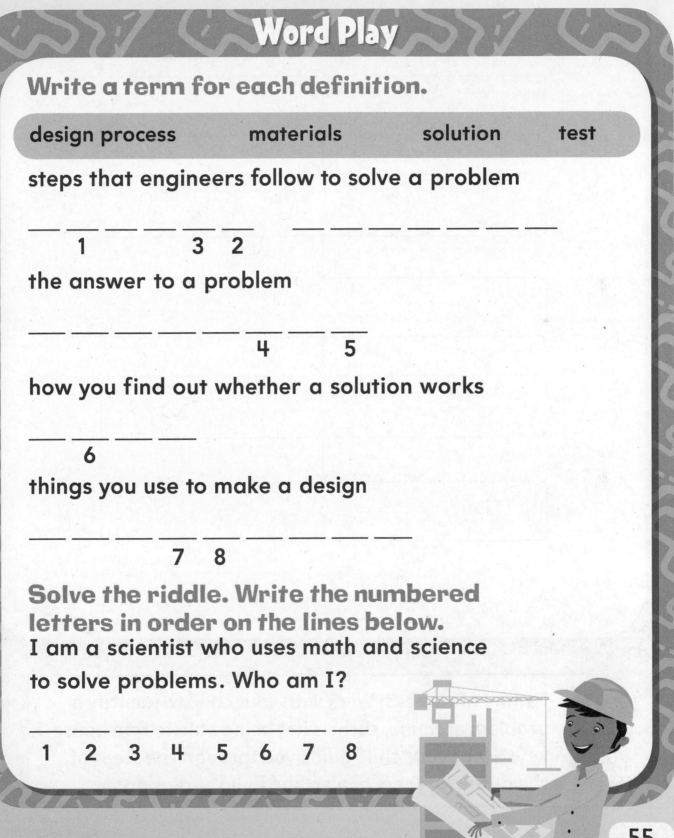

Complete the flowchart with the steps of the design process.

Design Process

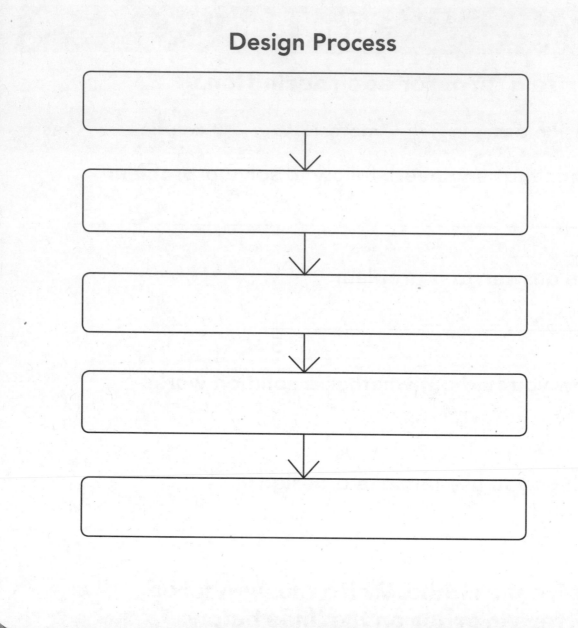

TEKS **2.2A** ask questions about organisms, objects, and events during observations and investigations **2.2B** plan and conduct descriptive investigations such as how organisms grow **2.2D** record and organize data using pictures, numbers, and words **2.2E** communicate observations and justify explanations using student-generated data from simple descriptive investigations **2.3A** identify and explain a problem in his/her own words and propose a task and solution for the problem such as lack of water in a habitat

Name _____

Essential Question

How Can We Use the Design Process?

Set a Purpose

Identify and explain the problem you want to solve.

_____

_____

Think About the Procedure

❶ Why do you need to plan your solution?

_____

_____

_____

❷ Why do you need to test your solution?

_____

_____

Record Your Data

Draw to communicate your solution and the test results. Label the materials. Write a caption to tell how your solution works.

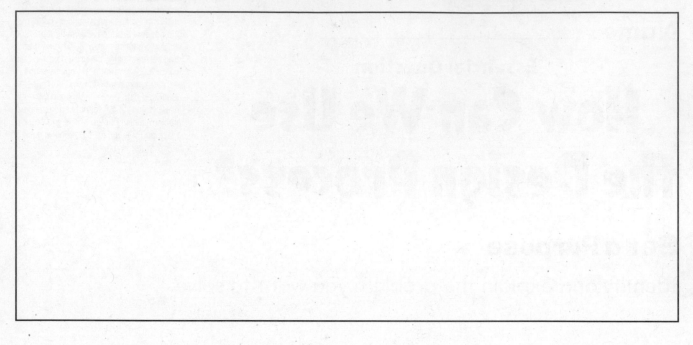

Draw Conclusions

How did the design process help you solve the problem?

_____

_____

Ask More Questions

What other questions could you ask about using the design process?

_____

_____

TEKS 2.3A identify and explain a problem in his/her own words and propose a task and solution for the problem such as lack of water in a habitat

Lesson **3**

Essential Question

What Is Technology?

Engage Your Brain!

Find the answer to the question in the lesson.

You use the technology in this picture every day. What is it?

It is a

_____ .

Active Reading

Lesson Vocabulary

1 Preview the lesson.

2 Write the 2 vocabulary terms here.

_____   _____

By Design

Did you use a toothbrush or turn on a light today? Both a toothbrush and a light are kinds of technology. **Technology** is what engineers make to meet needs and solve problems. Anything people design to help us do things is technology.

Active Reading

Find the sentence that tells the meaning of **technology**. Draw a line under the sentence.

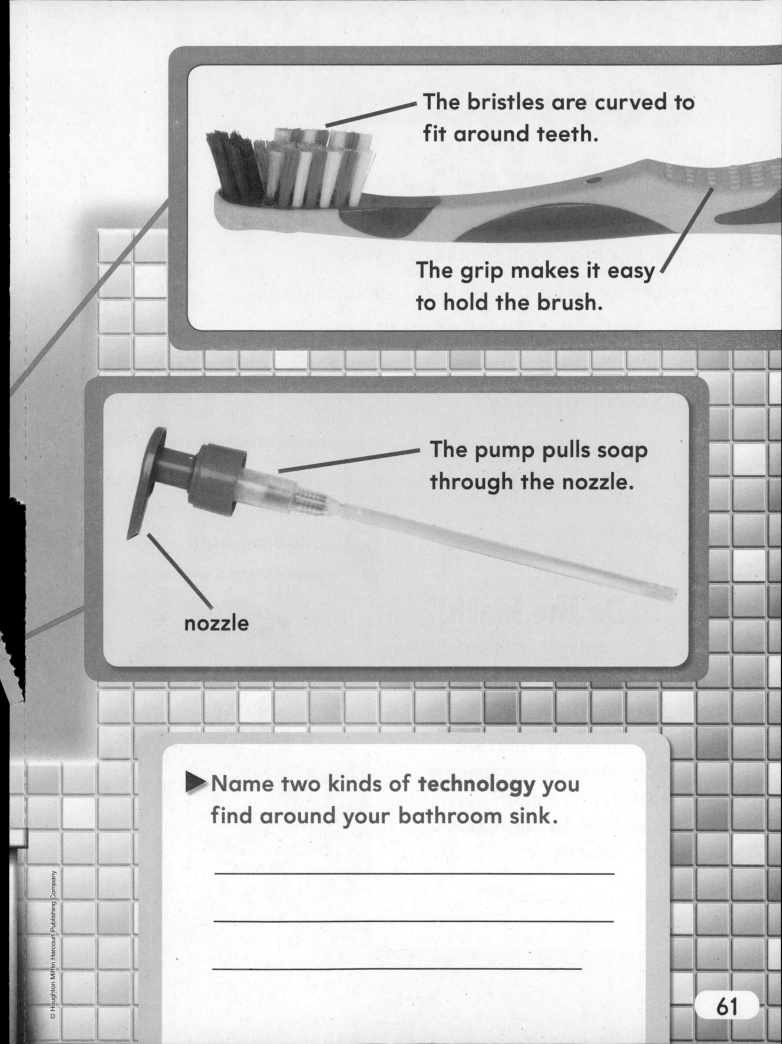

The bristles are curved to fit around teeth.

The grip makes it easy to hold the brush.

The pump pulls soap through the nozzle.

nozzle

▶ Name two kinds of **technology** you find around your bathroom sink.

_____

_____

_____

Everyday Technology

Technology is all around us. We use it every day. We depend on it at home and at school. Technology helps us do things. It helps us meet our needs. How have you used technology today?

Technology lights our homes. Electricity can produce light.

Do the Math!
Solve a Problem

Read the word problem. Answer the question.

The average person uses 80 gallons of water at home each day. How much water does a person use in 2 days? Show your work.

_____ gallons

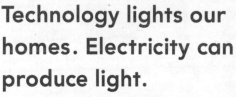

► When the power goes out, so do electric lights. What else could you do to light your home?

_____

_____

_____

Technology helps bring clean water to our homes.

Technology helps us make food. An oven, stovetop, and microwave oven cook food and heat water.

Play It Safe

Technology can be helpful when we use it with care. It can be unsafe if we do not use it with care.

We should use each kind of technology the way it was designed to be used. We should wear safety gear if we need to. Using technology correctly helps us stay safe.

Active Reading

The main idea is the most important idea about something. Draw two lines under the main idea.

The things that keep us safe are technology, too!

The hard plastic keeps things out of the eyes.

Foam and the hard covering protect the head.

Straps hold the helmet in place.

▶ What technology keeps you safe in a car?

_____

_____

_____

Environmental Effects

Technology can affect the environment. An **environment** is all the living and nonliving things in a place.

Batteries, for example, are a helpful technology. They provide power to phones, cars, toys, and other things. But they can harm the environment, too.

When old batteries break down, they can pollute water and soil.

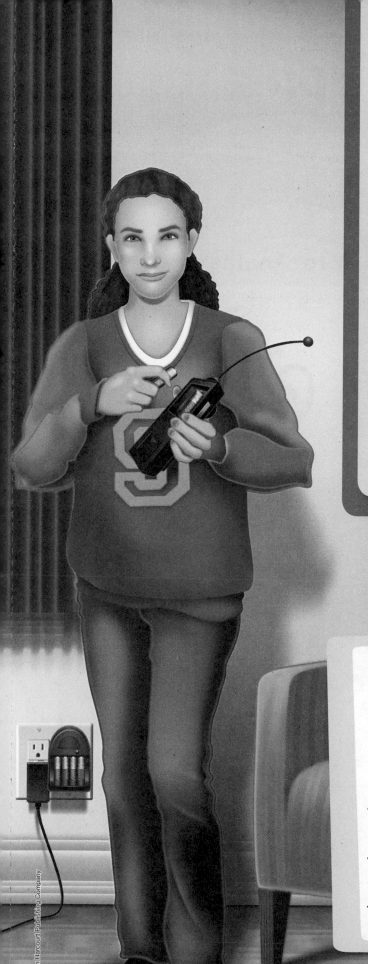

Some batteries can be used over and over again. Most batteries can be recycled. How do you think this helps the environment?

▶ Write two ways you can keep batteries from being thrown away.

_____

_____

_____

Sum It Up!

① Circle It!

Circle the examples of technology.

② Write It!

Write a way people depend on technology.

_____

_____

_____

③ Draw It

Draw a way you use technology to be safe.

Name _____

Word Play

Match each word to its meaning.

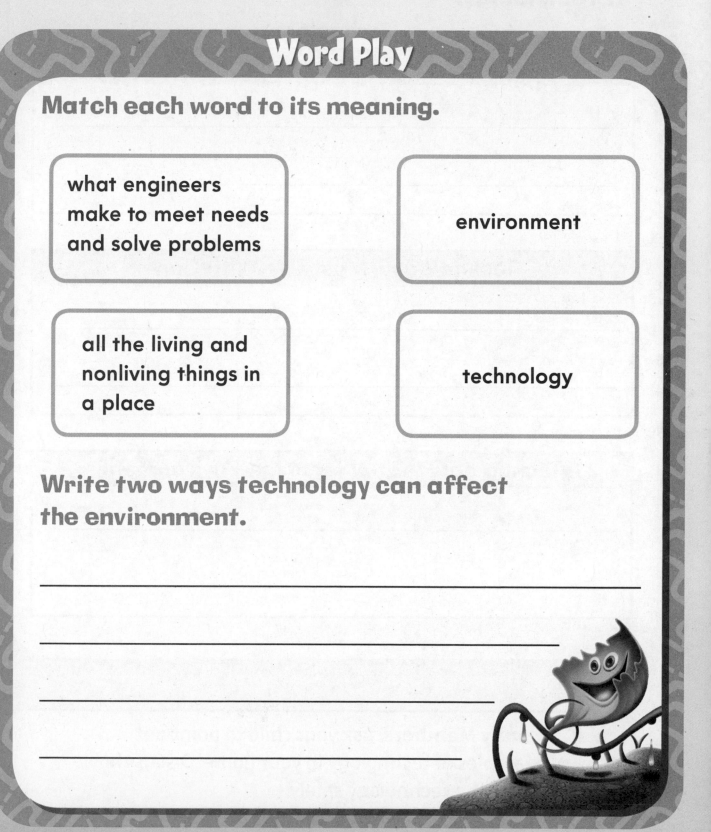

| what engineers make to meet needs and solve problems | environment |
| all the living and nonliving things in a place | technology |

Write two ways technology can affect the environment.

_____

_____

_____

_____

Apply Concepts

Fill in the chart. Write different kinds of technology.

Technology

Technology I Use Every Day
_____
_____

Technology I Must Use With Care
_____
_____

Technology That Affects the Environment
_____
_____

Take It Home!

Family Members: Ask your child to point out examples of technology in your home. Discuss how to use the technology safely.

TEKS **2.2A** ask questions about organisms, objects, and events during observations and investigations **2.2B** plan and conduct descriptive investigations such as how organisms grow **2.2D** record and organize data using pictures, numbers, and words **2.2E** communicate observations and justify explanations using student-generated data from simple descriptive investigations **2.3A** identify and explain a problem in his/her own words and propose a task and solution for the problem such as lack of water in a habitat

Name _____

Essential Question

How Can We Improve Technology?

Set a Purpose

Identify the problem you want to solve.

_____

_____

Think About the Procedure

❶ What are some objects you could choose?

_____

_____

❷ How could you improve your object?

_____

Record Your Data

Draw to communicate your solution. Label your picture.

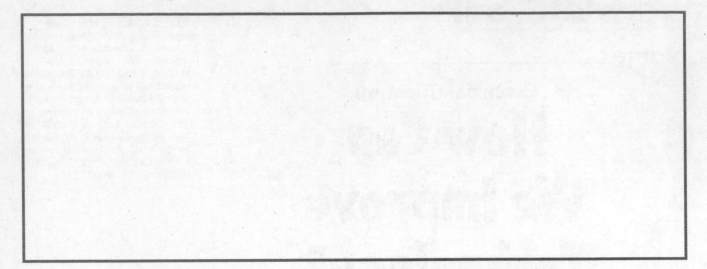

Draw Conclusions

How did your solution improve the object you chose?

_____

_____

_____

Ask More Questions

What other questions could you ask about improving your object?

_____

_____

_____

_____

Ask a Roller Coaster Designer

What do roller coaster designers do?
We design roller coasters for amusement parks. We think up ideas for new rides. We also figure out how much they will cost to build.

Do designers work alone?
We work as a team with engineers to make a design. The design has to work and be safe and fun for riders. A factory then builds the ride.

How long does it take to build a roller coaster?
It usually takes about a year from design to finish. A simpler design takes less time.

Now It's Your Turn!

▶ What question would you ask a roller coaster designer?

_____

_____

_____

_____

Design Your Own Roller Coaster

▶ Explore what a roller coaster designer does. Draw your own roller coaster in the space below.

▶ Explain your design. Write about how your roller coaster moves.

_____

_____

_____

Unit 2 Review

Name _____

Vocabulary Review

Use the terms in the box to complete the sentences.

> design process
> environment
> technology

TEKS 2.3C

1. A set of steps engineers follow to solve problems is a(n) _____.

TEKS 2.3C

2. What engineers make to meet needs and solve problems is _____.

3. All of the living and nonliving things in a place is a(n) _____.

Science Concepts

Fill in the letter of the choice that best answers the question.

TEKS 2.3C

4. Explore what different scientists do. What kind of work do engineers do?

   Ⓐ make new designs for people to buy

   Ⓑ invent new steps in the design process

   Ⓒ solve problems using math and science

TEKS 2.3A

5. What is a problem with using some kinds of technology?

   Ⓐ They can help people meet their needs.

   Ⓑ They can sometimes harm the environment.

   Ⓒ They are all around us and we use them every day.

TEKS 2.3A

6. You choose these items to design a solution to a problem.

What step of the design process do you propose to do?

Ⓐ Find a problem.

Ⓑ Plan and build.

Ⓒ Test and improve.

7. Which classroom object is an example of technology?

Ⓐ a pencil

Ⓑ a plant

Ⓒ a student

TEKS 2.3C

8. Why do engineers use the design process?

Ⓐ It is easy.

Ⓑ It helps them use tools.

Ⓒ It helps them solve problems.

9. Look at this object.

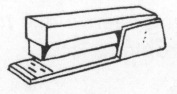

What is it an example of?

Ⓐ the design process

Ⓑ an engineer

Ⓒ technology

TEKS 2.3A

10. Omar wants to find a way to keep his pens from falling to the bottom of his backpack. Which task should he do first?

Ⓐ He should test a solution.

Ⓑ He should brainstorm a solution.

Ⓒ He should communicate a solution.

TEKS 2.3A

11. You are following the steps in the design process to propose a solution. How can you tell whether your solution works?

Ⓐ Ask other people.

Ⓑ Draw and write about the solution.

Ⓒ Test the solution.

TEKS 2.3A

12. How is this girl using technology to solve a problem?

Ⓐ She is using technology to stay clean.

Ⓑ She is using technology to stay safe.

Ⓒ She is using technology to get water.

Inquiry and the Big Idea
Write the answers to these questions.

TEKS 2.3A

13. You need a way to carry six drink cans or bottles at the same time. Explain the steps you would follow to design a tool to solve your problem.

1. _____

2. _____

3. _____

4. _____

5. _____

TEKS 2.3A

14. Look at the picture.

a. Identify how people use this technology.

_____

_____

b. What is good about this technology?

_____

c. What is bad about this technology?

_____

Changes in Matter

Big Idea

Matter has different properties. Matter can be classified and described by its properties. Properties of matter can change.

TEKS 2.2A, 2.2B, 2.2D, 2.2E, 2.2F, 2.3C, 2.5A, 2.5B, 2.5C, 2.5D

I Wonder Why

The floaties and the swim toys all keep their different shapes. Why?
Turn the page to find out.

Here's Why Gases take the shape of their container. This makes each object look different.

In this unit, you will explore this Big Idea, the Essential Questions, and the Investigations on the Inquiry Flipchart.

Levels of Inquiry Key ■ DIRECTED ■ GUIDED ■ INDEPENDENT

Track Your Progress

Big Idea Matter has different properties. Matter can be classified and described by its properties. Properties of matter can change.

Essential Questions

○ **Now I Get the Big Idea!**

Science Notebook

Before you begin each lesson, be sure to write your thoughts about the Essential Question.

TEKS **2.5A** classify matter by physical properties, including shape, relative mass, relative temperature, texture, flexibility, and whether material is a solid or a liquid

Lesson **1**

Essential Question

What Is Matter?

Engage Your Brain!

Find the answer to the question in the lesson.

What is inside the balloon?

Hot gas

Active Reading

Lesson Vocabulary

❶ Preview the lesson.

❷ Write the 7 vocabulary terms here.

_____   _____

_____   _____

_____   _____

_____

Matter Matters

All of the objects shown here are matter. **Matter** is anything that takes up space and has mass. **Mass** is the amount of matter in an object.

Active Reading

Find the sentence that tells the meaning of **mass**. Draw a line under the sentence.

Shape

These objects have different shapes. The ball is round. The plate is square.

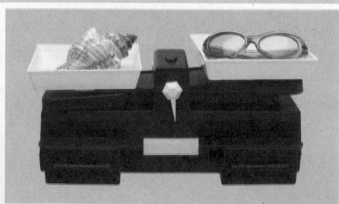

Mass

These objects have different masses. The shell has more mass than the sunglasses.

Matter has properties. A **property** is one part of what something is like. Some properties are shape, mass, temperature, flexibility, and texture.

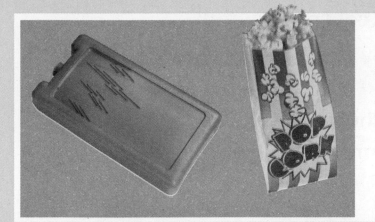

Temperature
These objects have different temperatures. The ice pack is cold. The popcorn is warm.

Flexibility
These objects have different flexibilities. The beach noodle can bend more than the cooler.

Texture
These shells have different textures. The pink shell is bumpy. The purple shell is smooth.

▶ **Name another object with a smooth texture.**

White border

Classify Matter

You can classify matter by its properties.
Think about an ice pack. It is cold and smooth.
You can classify an ice pack by these properties.

▶ Classify the objects by their properties. Circle your answers.

Shape

Which object is round?

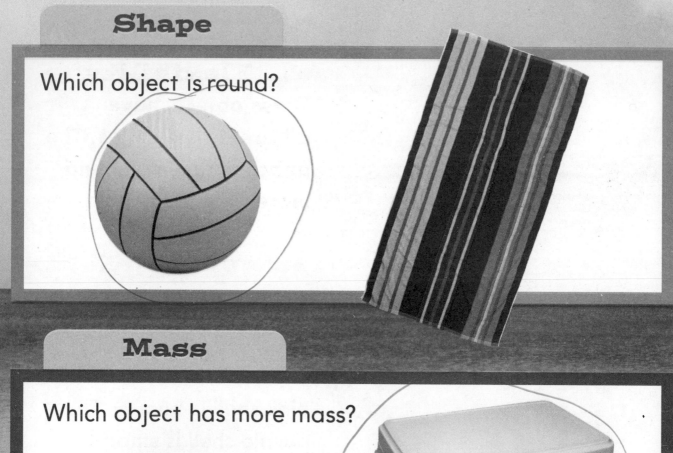

Mass

Which object has more mass?

Temperature

Which object is cold?

Flexibility

Which object is more flexible?

Texture

Which object is bumpy?

State of the Art

You can also classify matter by whether it is a solid, liquid, or gas. Solid, liquid, and gas are three states of matter. The boy's sunglasses are a solid. The water in his bottle is a liquid. The beach ball is filled with gases.

Active Reading

The main idea is the most important idea about something. Draw two lines under the main idea.

What two states of matter make up the beach ball?

Solid as a Rock

Look at the chair, the towel, and the hat. How are these objects the same? The answer is that all three are solids.

A **solid** is the only state of matter that has its own shape. You can measure the mass of a solid. What other solids do you see in this picture?

▶ Draw a solid object that you would take to the beach.

Shape Up!

Is juice a solid? No. It does not have its own shape. If you pour juice from a pitcher into a glass, the shape of the juice changes.

Juice is a liquid. A **liquid** is a state of matter that takes the shape of its container. You can measure the volume of a liquid. **Volume** is the amount of space that matter takes up.

▶ Compare the pitcher to the glass on its right. Which container has the larger volume?

Salt water is a kind of liquid.

Life's a Gas

This girl is blowing air into the beach ball. Air is made up of gases. A **gas** is a state of matter that fills all the space in its container. The air will keep spreading out until it fills the entire beach ball.

Active Reading

Find the sentence that tells the meaning of **gas**. Draw a line under the sentence.

You can't see air, but you can see and feel what it does.

What's the Matter?

Matter can be a solid, liquid, or gas. Which of these objects are solids? Which are liquids? Where are the gases?

► Classify each thing as a solid, liquid, or gas. Write your answer in the table.

pool water	chair	air in balls

Sum It Up!

1 Match It!

Draw lines to match each object with its state of matter.

solid

liquid

gas

2 Mark It!

Classify by properties. Draw an X on the object in each group that does not belong.

Brain Check

Name _____

Word Play

Write the word for each clue. Fill in the missing numbers in the table. Then decode the message.

a	b	c	d	e	f	g	h	i	j	k	l	m
11	26	4	16	8	25	9	13	23	6	14	20	19

n	o	p	q	r	s	t	u	v	w	x	y	z
7	18	1	3	22	21	17	2	15	10	5	12	24

takes the shape of its container

__l__ __i__ __q__ __u__ __i__ __d__
20 23 3 2 23 16

what something is like

__p__ __r__ __o__ __p__ __e__ __r__ __t__ __y__
1 22 18 1 8 22 17 12

matter with its own shape

__s__ __o__ __l__ __i__ __d__
21 18 20 23 16

the amount of matter in an object   __m__ __a__ __s__ __s__
19 11 21 21

__A__   __d__ __a__ __y__   __a__ __t__   __t__ __h__ __e__
11   16 11 12   11 17   17 13 8

__b__ __e__ __a__ __c__ __h__   __i__ __s__   __a__
26 8 11 4 13   23 21   11

__l__ __a__ __u__ __g__ __h__ __i__ __n__ __g__   __m__ __a__ __t__ __t__ __e__ __r__!
20 11 2 9 13 23 7 9   19 11 17 17 8 22

Apply Concepts

Look at the objects. Classify them by shape, mass, temperature, texture, and flexibility. Write or draw your answers.

rectangle	less mass	cold	smooth	less flexible

Take It Home!

Family Members: Look around your home and neighborhood. Work with your child to classify objects by shape, mass, temperature, texture, and flexibility.

TEKS 2.5B compare changes in materials caused by heating and cooling **2.5C** demonstrate that things can be done to materials to change their physical properties such as cutting, folding, sanding, and melting **2.5D** combine materials that when put together can do things that they cannot do by themselves such as building a tower or a bridge and justify the selection of those materials based on their physical properties

Lesson 2

Essential Question

How Does Matter Change?

🧠 Engage Your Brain!

Find the answer to the question in the lesson.

How did the water turn into ice?

Water becomes ice when heat
_____

Active Reading

Lesson Vocabulary

1 Preview the lesson.

2 Write the 2 vocabulary terms here.

_____ _____

A Material Change

The properties of materials can change.
Some ways we can change properties are by
cutting, folding, sanding, and melting.

Active Reading

The main idea is the most important idea about
something. Draw two lines under the main idea.

cutting

Cutting changes the shape and size of paper.

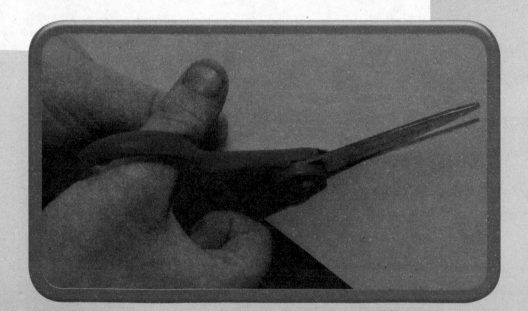

folding

Folding changes the shape and size of paper.

sanding

Sanding changes the texture of wood. It makes wood smoother. Sanding may also change the color of wood.

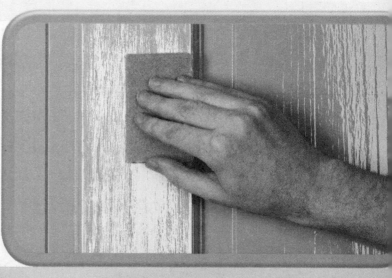

melting

Melting changes the size of ice cubes. When the ice cubes melt, they change from a solid to a liquid.

▶ Read the captions. Circle two changes sanding can make to wood.

Mix and Match

You can combine materials. Combined materials can do things that each material could not do alone. Properties help you choose which materials to use.

Sneaker Materials

This sneaker is made of rubber, canvas, cotton, and metal. The rubber is strong and protects the bottom of your foot. The cotton laces are flexible. You can tie them to keep the sneaker on. Each material by itself does not make the sneaker useful. You need all the materials combined.

cotton laces

canvas

metal loop

rubber sole

Making a Bike

A bike is also made of combined materials. Each material helps the bike work. Rubber is a good material for tires. It is strong and flexible.

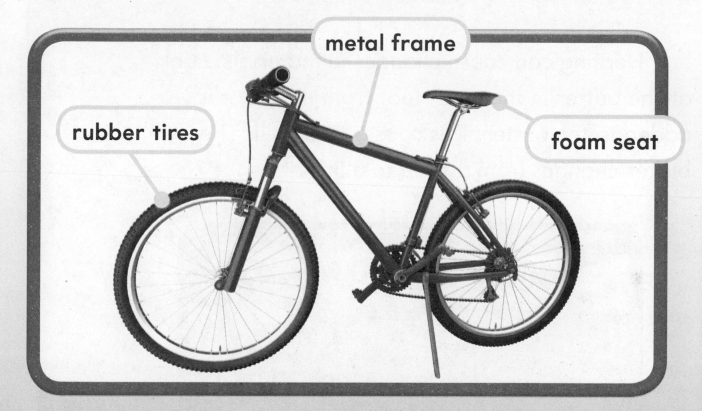

metal frame

rubber tires

foam seat

▶ Look at the materials that make up the bike. Why is foam a good material for a seat?

_____

_____

▶ Why is metal a good material for the frame?

_____

_____

Heat It Up!

Heating can cause changes to materials. Look at the butter in the pan. Heat from the stove is added to the butter. This causes it to melt. The butter changes from a solid to a liquid.

Heat melts butter.

Look at the water in the pot. As the stove heats the water, it evaporates. **Evaporation** is the change of water from a liquid to a gas. Water that is a gas is called **water vapor**.

What happens to an egg when you heat it? It does not evaporate or melt. Heat cooks the egg. The texture and color of the egg change.

An uncooked egg is runny and clear.

A cooked egg is firm and white.

▶ Compare how heating changes butter and an egg.

_____

_____

Cool It Down!

Cooling also causes changes to materials. Think about making juice pops. You put juice in a freezer to cool the juice. Heat is taken away. The juice freezes, or turns from a liquid to a solid. Other materials that will change from a liquid to a solid when they are cooled enough are water, milk, and tea.

Active Reading

An effect tells what happens. What happens when you cool juice in a freezer? Draw two lines under the effect.

Freezing changes liquid juice into a solid juice pop.

Cooling does not change all materials in the same way. Suppose you put a plastic bag in a freezer. It stays a solid. What happens when you take the bag out of the freezer? It will still be a solid.

In a freezer, the juice-pop tray does not change state. It gets colder. It might also bend a little.

▶ Compare the changes that happen to juice and a juice-pop tray when they are cooled in a freezer.

_____

_____

_____

Sum It Up!

① Circle It!

Circle what would change the color of wood.

cutting

sanding

folding

② Match It!

Draw lines to show if the material has been heated or cooled.

heated

cooled

③ Draw It!

Draw an object made of different materials. Write labels to show the materials.

Name _____

Word Play

Use the words in the word bank to complete the chart. Tell which properties are changed by each action. The words can be used more than once.

color	shape	size	state	texture

Cutting	Sanding	Folding	Melting
_____	_____	_____	_____
_____	_____	_____	_____
_____	_____	_____	_____
_____	_____	_____	_____
_____	_____	_____	_____

Apply Concepts

In each box, write a word or phrase that tells the cause of the effect.

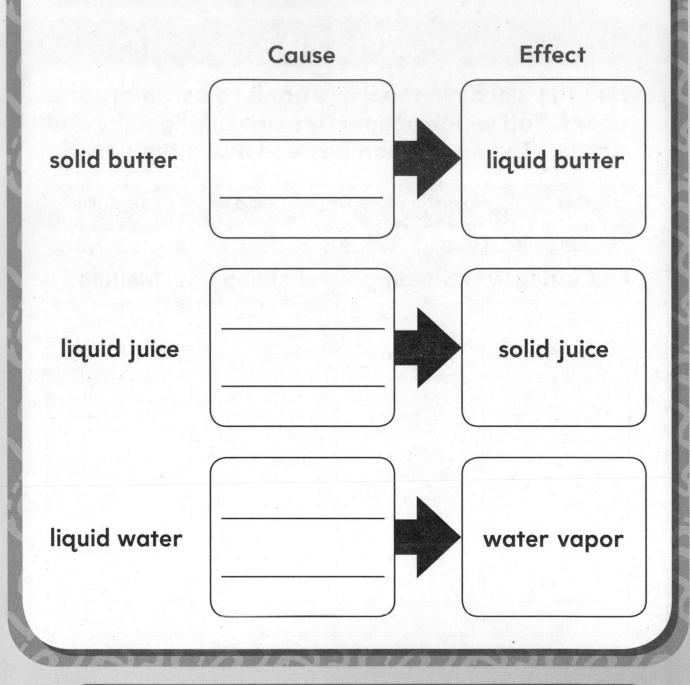

Cause   Effect

solid butter → _____ → liquid butter

liquid juice → _____ → solid juice

liquid water → _____ → water vapor

Take It Home!

Family Members: Have your child point out materials changing states at home, such as water freezing or food cooking. Ask him or her to explain how heating or cooling causes those changes.

TEKS 2.3A identify and explain a problem in his/her own words and propose a task and solution for the problem... 2.5D combine materials that when put together can do things that they cannot do by themselves such as building a tower or a bridge and justify the selection of those materials based on their physical properties

Cross That Bridge
Materials Matter

People combine materials to build things. When put together, the materials do things that they cannot do alone. Look at the Brooklyn Bridge. It was built with stone and steel. Stone was used because it is strong and lasts a long time. Steel was used because it is strong and flexible.

> The bridge towers are made of stone. The stone towers hold up the cables.

> The cables are made of steel. The steel cables hold up the part of the bridge where cars and people go.

> Stone and steel together make the bridge. Either material alone could not do the job.

Compare Materials

Look at the material used to build each house. Write a possible good thing and bad thing about each material.

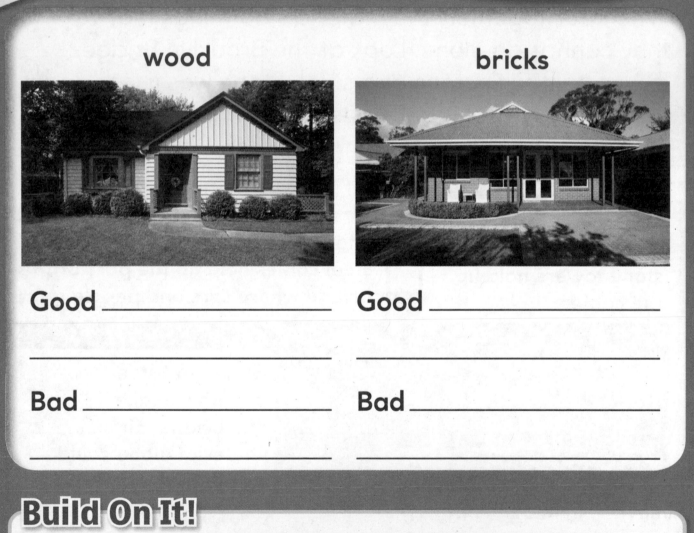

wood

bricks

Good _____

Good _____

_____

_____

Bad _____

Bad _____

_____

_____

Build On It!

Choose materials and design your own bridge or tower. Complete **Design It: Combine Materials** on the Inquiry Flipchart.

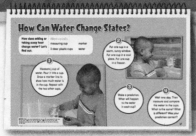

TEKS 2.2A ask questions about organisms, objects, and events during observations and investigations 2.2B plan and conduct descriptive investigations such as how organisms grow 2.2D record and organize data using pictures, numbers, and words 2.2E communicate observations and justify explanations using student-generated data from simple descriptive investigations 2.2F compare results of investigations with what students and scientists know about the world 2.5B compare changes in materials caused by heating and cooling

Name _____

Essential Question

How Can Water Change States?

Set a Purpose

Tell what you want to find out in this investigation.

_____

Make Predictions

What do you think will happen to the water?

_____

_____

_____

Think About the Procedure

Why do you measure the water at the beginning of the activity?
Why do you measure again at the end?

_____

_____

Record Your Data

Record the amount of water at the start. At the end, record your observations and measurements as possible.

	Warm Place	Cool Place	Freezer
Start			
End			

Draw Conclusions

Compare your results with what you predicted. How does heating and cooling affect water?

_____

_____

_____

Ask More Questions

What other questions could you ask about the ways water can change?

_____

_____

1

Dr. Chou was born in Taiwan. She studies physics. Physics is a science that tells about matter and energy.

2

She is a teacher at a university called Georgia Tech.

4

Things to Know About

Dr. Mei-Yin Chou

3

At Georgia Tech, Dr. Chou studies how gases affect solids.

4

She helps girls and women get involved in learning and teaching science.

Word Whiz

▶ Explore the work of Dr. Chou. Write the words to match the clues.

| Taiwan | physics | gases | women | Georgia Tech |

Across

3 Dr. Chou teaches at this university.

Down

1 Dr. Chou helps them learn about science.

2 This science tells about matter and energy.

4 Dr. Chou studies how these affect solids.

5 Dr. Chou was born in this country.

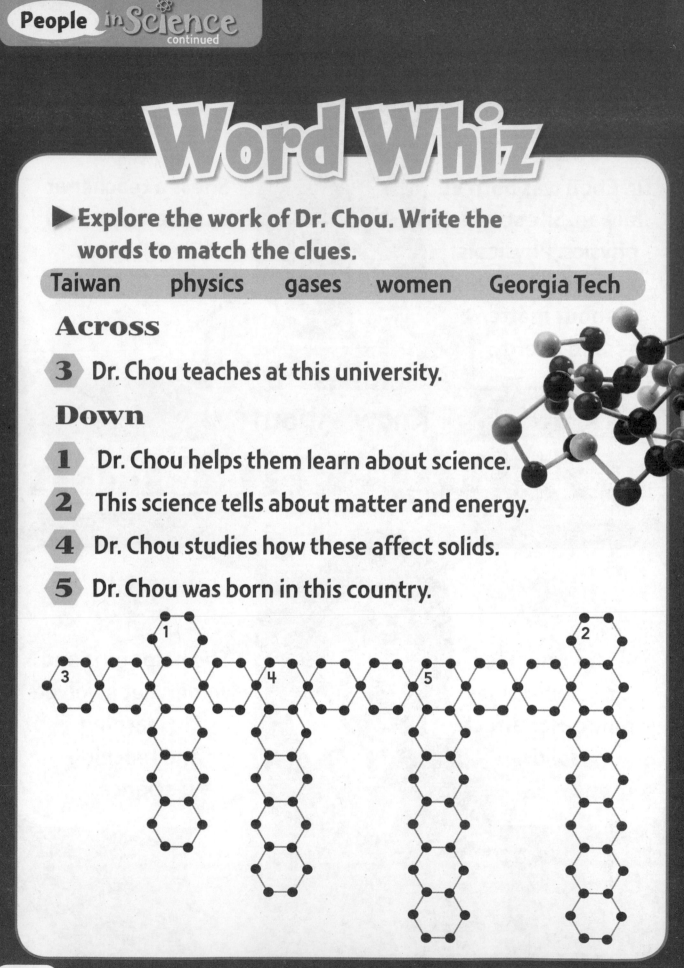

© Houghton Mifflin Harcourt Publishing Company   (t) ©Arville/Getty Images

Name _____

Vocabulary Review
Use the terms in the box to complete the sentences.

liquid
matter
property

TEKS 2.5A

1. A _____ is one part of what something is like.

TEKS 2.5A

2. Anything that has mass and takes up space is _____.

TEKS 2.5A

3. A state of matter that takes the shape of its container is a _____.

Science Concepts
Fill in the letter of the choice that best answers the question.

TEKS 2.5A

4. Vindra wants to classify objects by shape. She puts a soccer ball and an orange in one group. What else belongs in this group?

Ⓐ a round bead

Ⓑ a square block

Ⓒ a rectangular box

TEKS 2.5B

5. What happens to water when it freezes?

Ⓐ It becomes a gas.

Ⓑ It becomes a liquid.

Ⓒ It becomes a solid.

TEKS 2.5C

6. This boy is folding paper. Which properties of the paper is he changing?

Ⓐ size and shape

Ⓑ shape and texture

Ⓒ color and size

TEKS 2.5A

7. Classify these materials. Which is a solid?

Ⓐ a cloud

Ⓑ a penny

Ⓒ a puddle

TEKS 2.5B

8. How is the water changing?

Ⓐ It is melting.

Ⓑ It is evaporating.

Ⓒ It is condensing.

TEKS 2.5C

9. Jed wants to change the texture of a piece of wood. What should he do?

Ⓐ He should cut the wood.

Ⓑ He should fold the wood.

Ⓒ He should sand the wood.

TEKS 2.5A

10. Look at the properties of this object.

Which of these objects has about the same shape and texture?

Ⓐ

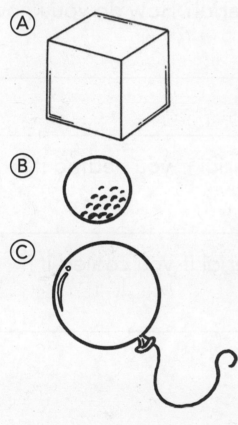

Ⓑ

Ⓒ

TEKS 2.5B

11. How does matter change when it melts?

Ⓐ It turns from a liquid to a gas.

Ⓑ It turns from a solid to a liquid.

Ⓒ It turns from a liquid to a solid.

TEKS 2.5D

12. Carl wants to combine materials to make a bike. Which material would be best to use for the bike's seat?

Ⓐ foam

Ⓑ metal

Ⓒ rubber

Inquiry and the Big Idea

Write the answers to these questions.

TEKS 2.2E, 2.5A, 2.5B

13. The same kind of matter is in these three containers.

a. What state of matter is the material? How do you know?

_____

_____

b. What would happen to the material if you heated it?

_____

c. What would happen to the material if you cooled it?

_____

Energy, Motion, and Magnets

heating glass

Big Idea

There are different forms of energy. Forces cause change.

TEKS 2.2A, 2.2B, 2.2D, 2.2E, 2.3C, 2.4A, 2.6A, 2.6B, 2.6C, 2.6D

I Wonder Why

This man is using heat to shape the glass. Why?

Turn the page to find out.

Here's Why Adding heat to the glass causes the glass to bend. Then the man can bend the glass into the shape he wants.

In this unit, you will explore this Big Idea, the Essential Questions, and the Investigations on the Inquiry Flipchart.

Levels of Inquiry Key ■ DIRECTED ■ GUIDED ■ INDEPENDENT

Track Your Progress

Big Idea There are different forms of energy. Forces cause change.

Essential Questions

Now I Get the Big Idea!

Science Notebook

Before you begin each lesson, be sure to write your thoughts about the Essential Question.

© Houghton Mifflin Harcourt Publishing Company (tr) ©Jim West/Alamy (inset) ©satit_srihin/Alamy (border) ©NDsc/Age Fotostock

TEKS **2.6A** investigate the effects on an object by increasing or decreasing amounts of light, heat, and sound energy such as how the color of an object appears different in dimmer light or how heat melts butter

Lesson **1**

Essential Question

What Is Energy?

Engage Your Brain!

Find the answer to the question in the lesson.

What kind of energy do you see in this picture?

_____ *energy*

Active Reading

Lesson Vocabulary

① Preview the lesson.

② Write the 7 vocabulary terms here.

_____ _____

_____ _____

_____ _____

_____

Full of Energy

Look at the fireworks over the city. They give off heat, light, and sound. Heat, light, and sound are kinds of energy. **Energy** is something that can cause matter to move or change.

Active Reading

A detail is a fact about a main idea. Draw one line under a detail. Draw an arrow to the main idea it tells about.

Sound is energy you can hear.

Light is energy that lets you see. You can see objects when light shines on them. You can also see objects that give off light.

Heat is a kind of energy that makes things warmer.

▶ Read the captions. Circle the name of the energy that makes things warmer. Underline the name of the energy that helps you see. Draw an X on the name of the energy you can hear.

121

Turn Up the Heat

You can feel heat from many things. Heat from the sun warms Earth. Moving things that rub together give off heat. Rubbing your hands together warms them up. Burning fuel gives off heat. Some fuels cook food and heat homes.

Adding heat warms objects. Taking away heat cools objects.

Adding heat causes the marshmallow to toast and change color.

As the fire dies down, heat is taken away and the family gets cooler.

▶ What happens when you add heat to objects?

_____

▶ What happens when you take heat away from objects?

_____

123

See the Light

The sun, electric lights, and fire all give
off light. Light is energy that lets you see. The
amount of light can change how you see things.
The amount of light can change how you
see the color of an object. Adding more light
can make an object look brighter. Taking away
light can make an object look dimmer.

How Much Light?

Different materials let different amounts of
light pass through.

A window pane
lets all light
pass through.

A lampshade
lets some light
pass through.

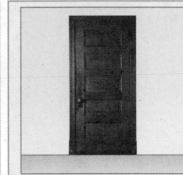

A door lets
no light pass
through.

▶ **Name something else that lets
no light pass through.**

_____

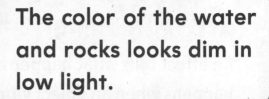

The color of the water and rocks looks dim in low light.

The color of the water and rocks looks bright in bright light.

Blow a horn. Clash cymbals. Clap your hands. What happens? You hear sound. Sound is energy you can hear.

Sound is made when an object vibrates. To **vibrate** is to move back and forth very quickly.

Active Reading

An effect tells what happens. What happens when an object vibrates? Draw two lines under the effect.

Pitch is how high or low a sound is. Instruments have different pitches. A whistle makes a sound with a high pitch. A big drum makes a sound with a low pitch.

Cheers from a crowd are loud. Whispers are soft. **Loudness** is how loud or soft a sound is. It takes more energy to make a loud sound than a soft sound.

▶ What happens to the loudness of a sound when more energy is used to make the sound?

_____

Sum It Up!

① Write It!

Name three kinds of energy.

_____

_____

_____

② Circle It!

Circle the answer.

What happens when you add heat to an object?

It gets cooler.

It gets warmer.

③ Match It!

Match each picture to the kind of energy it shows. A picture may show two kinds of energy.

sound   heat   light

Name _____

Word Play

Write a word from the word bank for each clue.

energy	loudness	heat	vibrate

1 how loud or soft a sound is ⬭(1)_ _ _ _ _ _ _

2 to move back and forth very quickly _ ⬭(2) _ _ _ _ _

3 can cause matter to move or change _ _ _ _ _ ⬭(3) _

4 energy that makes things warmer ⬭(4) _ _ _ ⬭(5) _

Solve the riddle. Write the circled letters in order on the lines below.

I am energy that lets you see. What am I?

_ _ _ _ _
1 2 3 4 5

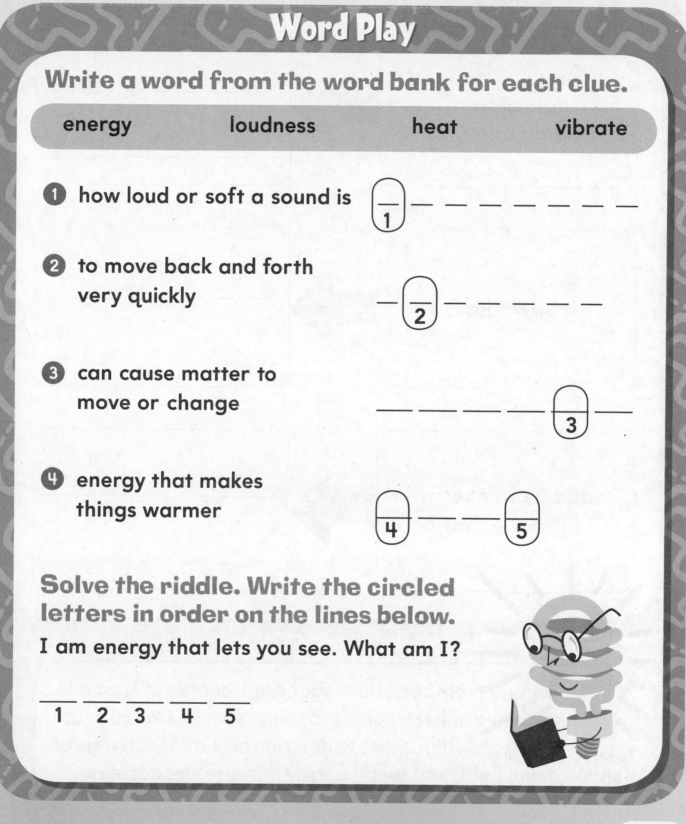

Apply Concepts

Fill in the chart. Write the effect of each cause.

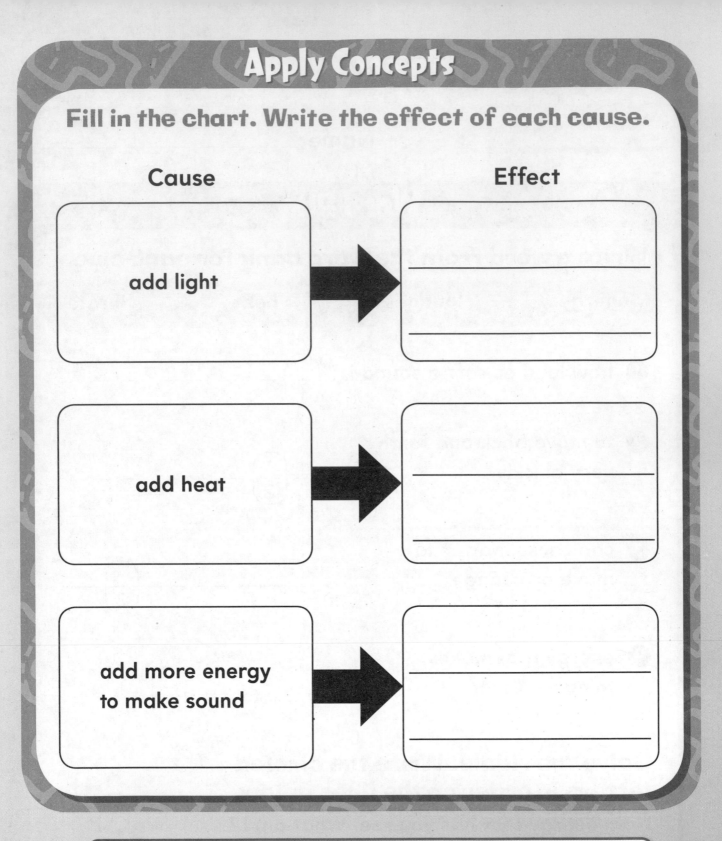

Cause   Effect

add light

add heat

add more energy
to make sound

Family Members: Have your child identify at least one example of heat, light, and sound energy around your home. Ask him or her to describe how things change as heat, light, and sound energy increase and decrease.

Take It Home!

Name _____

TEKS **2.2A** ask questions about organisms, objects, and events during observations and investigations **2.2B** plan and conduct descriptive investigations such as how organisms grow **2.2D** record and organize data using pictures, numbers, and words **2.2E** communicate observations and justify explanations using student-generated data from simple descriptive investigations **2.6A** investigate the effects on an object by increasing or decreasing amounts of light, heat, and sound energy such as how the color of an object appears different in dimmer light or how heat melts butter

Essential Question

How Does the Sun Warm Our Homes?

Set a Purpose

Explain what you will learn from this activity.

_____

State Your Hypothesis

Write your hypothesis, or statement that you will test.

_____

_____

Think About the Procedure

Why do you need to measure the temperature both outside the model and inside the model?

_____

_____

Record Your Data

Use your data to communicate your observations.

Place	Temperature at Start	Temperature After 1 Hour
Inside the Model		
Outside the Model		

Draw Conclusions

1 How does the sun warm our homes as the amount of heat increases?

_____

_____

2 How does the model help you draw a conclusion?

_____

_____

Ask More Questions

What are some other questions you could ask about how the sun warms our homes?

_____

_____

4 Things to Know About

Dr. Lawnie Taylor

1 Dr. Taylor studied physics. Physics is a science that tells about matter and energy.

2 He worked for the U.S. Department of Energy for many years.

3 He studied ways to use the sun's energy to heat homes and produce electricity.

4 Dr. Taylor also studied ways to use the sun's energy to make machines run.

Let the Sun Shine!

Explore the kind of work Dr. Taylor did. You can study solar energy, too!

▶ Write the number of each description next to the correct picture.

1 Solar panels on a house collect the sun's energy to produce electricity or heat water.

2 A solar farm can change the sun's energy into electricity for many people to use.

3 A solar car uses the sun's energy to make it run.

▶ How have you seen solar energy used?

_____

_____

Essential Question

What Are Forces?

Engage Your Brain!

Find the answer to the question in the lesson.

Is the circus star pushing or pulling on the chairs?

He is _____ on the chairs.

Active Reading

Lesson Vocabulary

1 Preview the lesson.

2 Write the 3 vocabulary terms here.

_____   _____

_____

In Full Force

This rope is moving around and around. It is in motion. **Motion** means movement. Something that is moving is in motion.

A juggler makes rings move in different ways. The juggler uses forces to change their motion. A **force** is a push or a pull. How do you use forces to change motion?

Active Reading

Find the sentence that tells the meaning of **force**. Draw a line under the sentence.

A **push** is a force that moves something away from you. A **pull** is a force that moves something toward you.

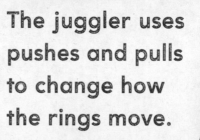

The juggler uses pushes and pulls to change how the rings move.

▶ Draw a push or a pull.

Up to Speed

How do acrobats fly through the air? They use forces to change their speed and direction. **Speed** is how fast something moves. A small force changes an object's speed and direction a little. A large force can change them a lot.

> The acrobats are using forces to change direction.

▶ **What happens to the speed of the cart if you give it a big push?**

_____

_____

► Draw a force changing the speed or direction of an object.

The harder the acrobats push and pull, the faster they go.

On the Move

Objects can move in different ways.
They can roll, spin, and slide. Rolling, spinning,
and sliding are patterns of movement. Look at
the pictures. Compare the patterns of movement.

Active Reading

A detail is a fact about a main idea. Draw
a line under a detail. Draw an arrow to the
main idea it tells about.

rolling

The unicyclist is rolling backward!
Rolling turns an object over and
over along a surface. It moves
an object to a new place.

spinning

Look at the plates spinning around on the poles. Spinning turns an object around and around in the same place.

sliding

The barrel is sliding across the floor. Sliding moves an object across a surface. The object does not turn. Sliding moves an object to a new place.

► Compare spinning, rolling, and sliding. Which kinds of motion move an object to a new place? Circle the caption heads.

Sum It Up!

1 Label It!

Compare the patterns of movement.
Write a label to name each one.

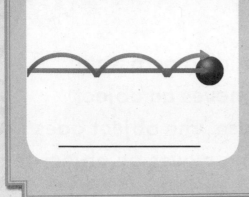

_____   _____   _____

2 Circle It!

Circle the answer.

Jay pushes a box with a little force. Then he pushes it with a lot more force. How will he change the box's speed?

The box goes _____ faster.

much   a little

3 Solve It!

Write the answer to the riddle.

I can be a push or a pull. I can change the motion of a ball, a boot, or even a bull!
What am I?

_____

Name _____

Word Play

Write a word from the box for each definition.

| spinning | speed | rolling | motion |

1 tells how fast something moves ___ ___ ___ ___(4)___

2 motion that turns an
object around and around (1)___ ___ ___ ___ ___ ___(7)

3 motion that turns an
object over and over ___ (2)___ (5)___ ___

4 when something moves ___ (3)___ (6)___

Solve the riddle. Write the circled letters
in order on the lines below.

I can move an object across
a surface. What am I?

___ ___ ___ ___ ___ ___ ___
1   2   3   4   5   6   7

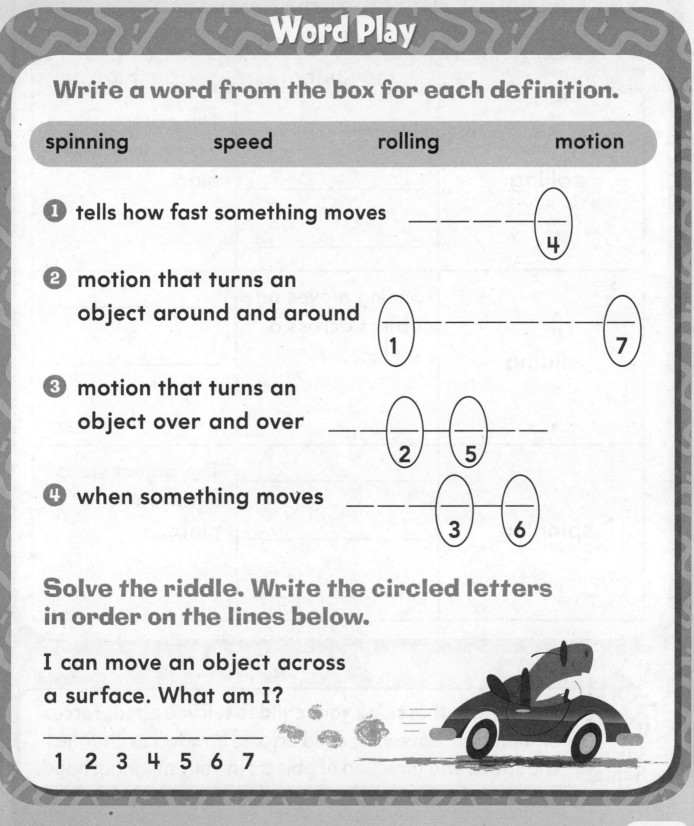

143

Apply Concepts

Compare rolling, sliding, and spinning. Describe each pattern of movement. Tell what happens to the position of the object that moves.

Patterns of Movement

	movement	position
rolling	_____ _____ _____	The object moves to a new place.
sliding	Sliding moves an object across a surface.	_____ _____ _____
spinning	_____ _____ _____	The object stays in the same place.

TEKS **2.2A** ask questions about organisms, objects, and events during observations and investigations **2.2B** plan and conduct descriptive investigations such as how organisms grow **2.2D** record and organize data using pictures, numbers, and words **2.2E** communicate observations and justify explanations using student-generated data from simple descriptive investigations **2.6C** trace the changes in the position of an object over time such as a cup rolling on the floor and a car rolling down a ramp

Name _____

Essential Question

How Do Forces Make Objects Move?

Set a Purpose

Write what you want to find out.

_____

_____

State Your Hypothesis

Write your hypothesis, or the statement that you will test.

_____

_____

Think About the Procedure

How does measuring time tell you how quickly an object moves from one position to another?

_____

_____

Record Your Data

Use your data to communicate your observations.

Force	Amount of Time
less force	
more force	

Draw Conclusions

1 How does the amount of time change when the force is greater?

_____

_____

2 How does the speed change when the force is greater?
Use your data to tell how you know.

_____

_____

Ask More Questions

What other questions can you ask about how force changes the motion of objects?

_____

_____

TEKS 2.4A collect, record, and compare information using tools, including...rulers...magnets
2.6B observe and identify how magnets are used in everyday life

Essential Question

What Are Magnets?

Engage Your Brain!

Find the answer to the question in the lesson.

What objects are making this smiley face?

_____

Active Reading

Lesson Vocabulary

❶ Preview the lesson.

❷ Write the 4 vocabulary terms here.

_____ _____

_____ _____

MAGNETIC PULL

A **magnet** is an object that can pull things made of iron and steel. A magnet can push or pull other magnets.

A magnet has two poles. A **pole** is a place on a magnet where the pull is the greatest. One pole is the north-seeking, or **N**, pole. The other pole is the south-seeking, or **S**, pole.

Active Reading

Find the sentence that tells the meaning of **pole**.
Draw a line under the sentence.

bar magnet

horseshoe magnet

ring magnets

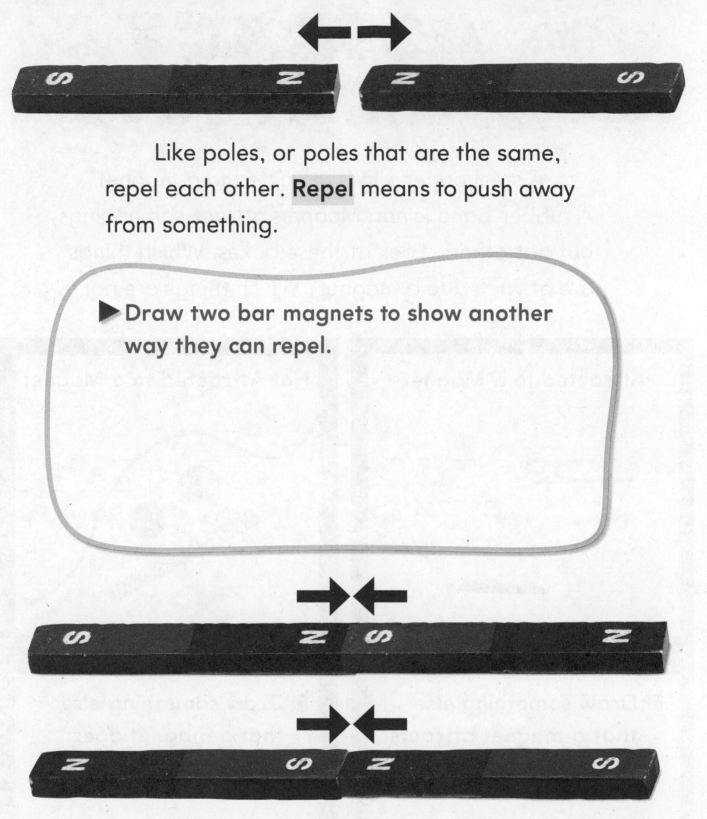

Like poles, or poles that are the same, repel each other. **Repel** means to push away from something.

▶ Draw two bar magnets to show another way they can repel.

Opposite poles, or poles that are different, attract each other. **Attract** means to pull toward something.

ATTRACT ATTENTION

A steel paper clip is attracted to a magnet. A rubber band is not. Magnets attract some things but not others. Look at these boxes. Which things are attracted to a magnet? Which things are not?

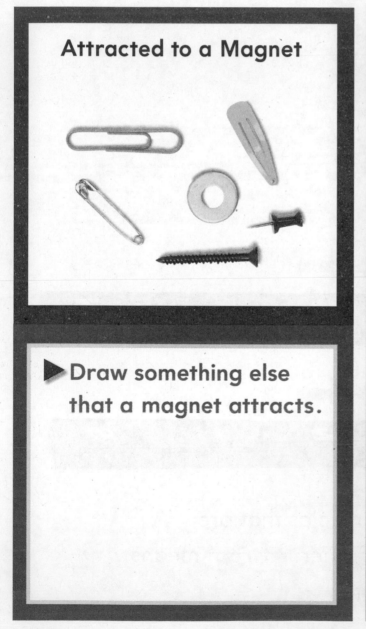

Attracted to a Magnet

Not Attracted to a Magnet

▶ Draw something else that a magnet attracts.

▶ Draw something else that a magnet does not attract.

150

Look at the way the magnet pulls the paper clips right through the hand! A magnet does not have to touch an object to move it. This is possible because of its magnetic field. This is the area around a magnet where the magnetic force is felt.

Do the Math!
Measuring Distance

How far from a paper clip must a magnet be before it does not attract it? Use a ruler to measure.

Distance	Did the magnet attract the paper clip?
½ inch	
1 inch	
1½ inches	
2 inches	

Compare the distances. How far from the magnet can you observe the magnetic field? How do you know?

_____

_____

MAGNETS EVERYWHERE

Magnets do much more than stick papers to the refrigerator. They help us in amazing ways! Look at the pictures. Observe how magnets are used everyday.

Active Reading

A detail is a fact about a main idea. Reread the captions. Draw one line under each of three details about how magnets are used.

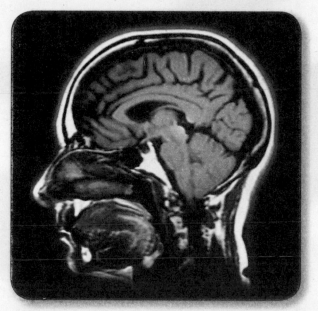

Magnets in MRI machines help make pictures of the inside of our bodies.

Huge magnets help sort items made of iron and steel before they are recycled.

▶ Identify how you use magnets everyday. Draw one way.

A Maglev train uses magnets to lift and move the train forward. One train has gone 361 miles per hour!

Sum It Up!

① Circle It!

Circle the objects a magnet attracts.

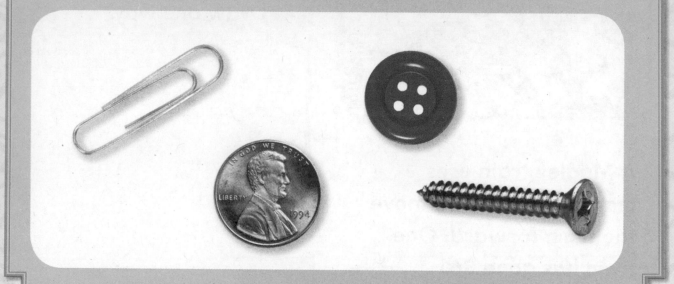

② Answer It!

Circle <u>true</u> or <u>false</u> to describe the statement.

A magnet must touch an object to attract it.

true   false

③ Draw It!

Draw a way you can use a magnet.

Name _____

Word Play

Write a word from the word bank on each line to complete the friendly letter.

magnets	poles	attract	repel

Dear Uncle Herbie,

Thanks for the science kit! I like the

_____ the best. They make some

objects move without touching them. I used

the big magnet to _____ an iron nail.

Each magnet has two places where

the pull is the strongest. These places are

called _____. When two poles that

are the same are pointed toward each other,

they _____. They push apart really hard.

Your niece,

Olivia

Apply Concepts

Complete this graphic organizer. Write an important detail about magnets in each box.

Magnets

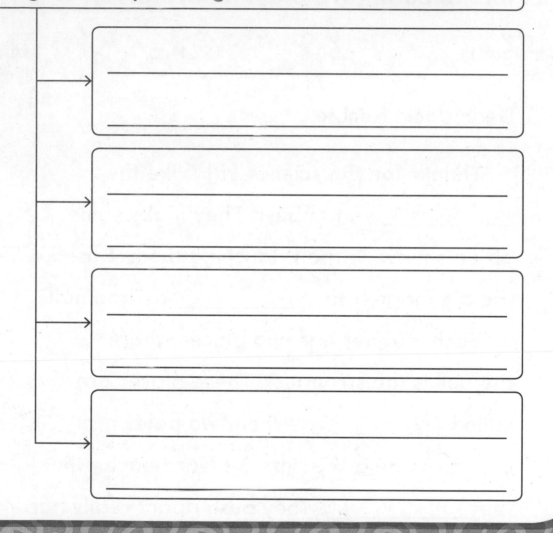

A magnet is an object that can push and pull other magnets and pull things made of iron and steel.

Magnets All Around

Everyday Magnets

Observe how magnets are used in everyday things.

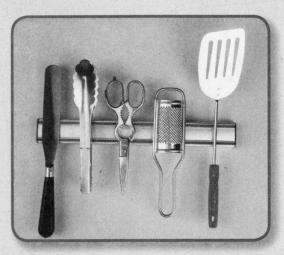

A magnet keeps these kitchen tools in order.

The magnet on this toy fishing rod attracts the metal fish to the magnet's surface.

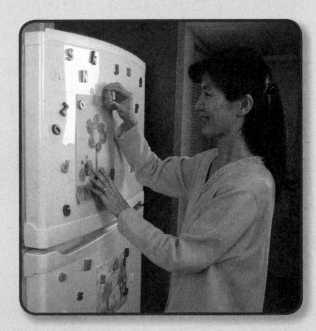

Magnets help keep the refrigerator door closed. They also attach the magnetic letters to the door.

Classroom Magnets

Identify how magnets are used everyday. Draw two ways that magnets are used in your classroom.

If you did not have magnets in your classroom, how would you do the things above that you drew?

_____

_____

Build On It!

Find your own way to use magnets. Complete **Design It: Use Magnets** on the Inquiry Flipchart.

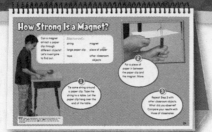
TEKS **2.2A** ask questions about organisms, objects, and events during observations and investigations **2.2B** plan and conduct descriptive investigations such as how organisms grow **2.2D** record and organize data using pictures, numbers, and words **2.2E** communicate observations and justify explanations using student-generated data from simple descriptive investigations **2.4A** collect, record, and compare information using tools, including . . . magnets . . .

Name _____

Essential Question

How Strong Is a Magnet?

Set a Purpose

Write what you want to find out.

_____

_____

State Your Hypothesis

Write your hypothesis, or the statement that you will test.

_____

_____

Think About the Procedure

Why is it important to test the strength of the magnet with different classroom objects?

_____

_____

Record Your Data

Communicate your observations in this chart. Write the names of the three objects you tested. Circle **attracts** or **does not attract** based on your results.

Object	Attracts/Does Not Attract	
piece of paper	attracts	does not attract
object 2	attracts	does not attract
object 3	attracts	does not attract
object 4	attracts	does not attract

Draw Conclusions

❶ How does putting something between the magnet and the paper clip affect the strength of the magnet?

_____

_____

❷ Why do you think that happens?

_____

Ask More Questions

What other questions can you ask about magnets?

_____

Unit 4 Review

Vocabulary Review

Use the terms in the box to complete the sentences.

> energy
> pitch
> pole

TEKS 2.6B

1. The place on a magnet where the pull is greatest is the _____.

TEKS 2.6A

2. Something that can cause matter to move or change is _____.

TEKS 2.6A

3. How high or low a sound seems is called _____.

Science Concepts

Fill in the letter of the choice that best answers the question.

TEKS 2.6A

4. What happens to the temperature inside a model home when you increase the amount of heat on the home?

   Ⓐ The temperature rises.

   Ⓑ The temperature falls.

   Ⓒ The temperature stays the same.

TEKS 2.6A

5. What kind of energy results when an object vibrates?

   Ⓐ heat

   Ⓑ light

   Ⓒ sound

TEKS 2.6C

6. What happens if you use a small force to push a large, heavy wagon?

ⓐ It moves very fast.

ⓑ It moves a lot.

ⓒ It moves a little.

TEKS 2.6B

7. Which of these objects can a magnet attract?

ⓐ

ⓑ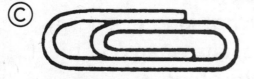

ⓒ

TEKS 2.6C

8. Look at the picture. Track the position of the ball. Suppose nothing stops the ball from rolling. In which position will the ball eventually stop?

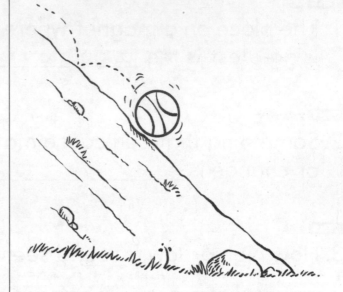

ⓐ at the top of the hill

ⓑ at the bottom of the hill

ⓒ in the middle of the hill

TEKS 2.6D

9. Compare the patterns of movement. Which tells what happens when an object turns over and over along a surface?

ⓐ rolling

ⓑ sliding

ⓒ spinning

10. How does decreasing light on an object change the way the object looks?

Ⓐ It makes the object look brighter.

Ⓑ It makes the object look dimmer.

Ⓒ It does not change the way the object looks.

11. What kind of motion is this top showing?

Ⓐ rolling

Ⓑ sliding

Ⓒ spinning

12. You blow softly on a ball. The ball crosses a finish line in 8 seconds. You blow hard on the ball. The ball crosses the finish line in 3 seconds. Which of the following can you infer from the activity?

Ⓐ The amount of force affects motion.

Ⓑ The amount of force does not affect motion.

Ⓒ You cannot use force to move an object.

Inquiry and the Big Idea
Write the answers to these questions.

TEKS 2.6A

13. What are three kinds of energy? Name each kind of energy, and tell what happens to an object when you increase that kind of energy.

a. _____

_____

b. _____

_____

c. _____

_____

TEKS 2.6B

14. Identify two ways magnets are used in everyday life.

_____

_____

_____

_____

UNIT 5
Earth and Its Resources

Big Idea

The natural world includes earth materials.

TEKS 2.1C, 2.2A, 2.2B, 2.2D, 2.3C, 2.7A, 2.7B, 2.7C

pecan trees
in Texas

I Wonder Why
People need natural resources. Why?
Turn the page to find out.

Here's Why People need natural resources for food. They need natural resources to make and build things.

In this unit, you will explore this Big Idea, the Essential Questions, and the Investigations on the Inquiry Flipchart.

Levels of Inquiry Key ■ DIRECTED ■ GUIDED ■ INDEPENDENT

Track Your Progress

Big Idea The natural world includes earth materials.

Essential Questions

Now I Get the Big Idea!

Science Notebook

Before you begin each lesson, be sure to write your thoughts about the Essential Question.

© Houghton Mifflin Harcourt Publishing Company

Essential Question

What Are Rocks?

Engage Your Brain!

Find the answer to the question in the lesson.

Where can you find rocks?

Rocks are all

over _____.

Active Reading

Lesson Vocabulary

❶ Preview the lesson.

❷ Write the 2 vocabulary terms here.

_____   _____

Rocks Rock!

Earth is made up of rock. A **rock** is a hard, nonliving object from the ground. Rocks can be different sizes. A boulder is a very large rock. A pebble is a very small rock. Sand is made of many tiny pieces of rock.

boulder

sand

▶ Look at the picture of the boulder and children. Describe the size of the boulder.

_____

Weathering changes big rocks into smaller rocks. **Weathering** is what happens when wind and water break down rock into smaller pieces.

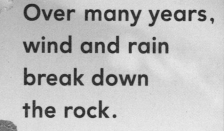

This cliff is made of rock.

Over many years, wind and rain break down the rock.

Active Reading

A cause tells why something happens. Read the captions. Why does rock break down? Draw one line under the cause.

Great Rock Groups

Rocks are made up of minerals. All rocks do not look and feel the same. They have different minerals and form in different ways. Look at the rocks. Observe the rocks by size, shape, color, and texture.

Size

Rocks can be different sizes. They can be as large as a boulder or as small as a grain of sand.

Shape

Rocks can be different shapes. They might be shaped like a circle, square, or rectangle.

▶ Choose a rock from this page. Describe its size, shape, color, and texture.

_____

_____

Color and Texture

Rocks can be different colors. Rocks can have different textures, too. They might feel smooth or rough.

Rock Resources

People use rocks every day. We use rocks to build things like walls and homes. We use rocks to make art. Rocks are very helpful!

This home and wall are made of rock.

This sculpture
is made of rock.

Do the Math!

Read the word problem.
Answer the questions.

Mike observes a brown rock
and a gray rock in his yard.
The brown rock weighs
11 pounds. The gray rock
weighs 13 pounds.

1. Use > and < to compare
   the weights of the rocks.

   _____ > _____

   _____ < _____

2. Which rock is heavier?

   the _____ rock

▶ Draw one way people use rocks.

① Compare It!

Observe the rocks. Describe the rocks by size, texture, and color.

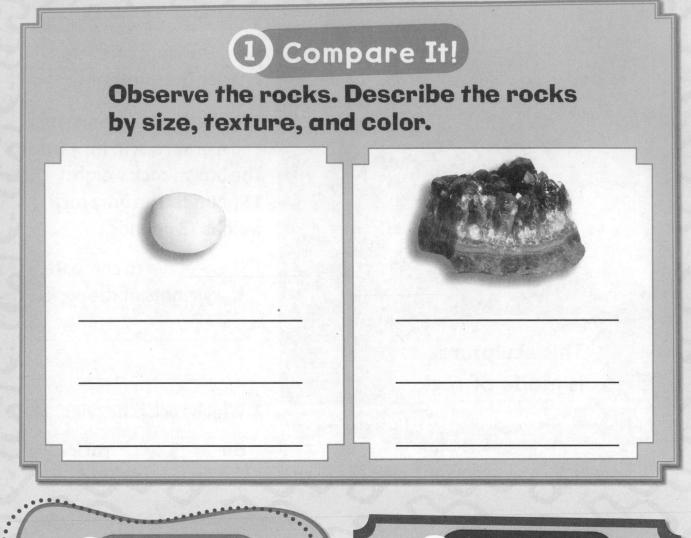

_____

_____

_____

_____

② Write It!

Where can you see rocks around your home? Explain.

_____

_____

③ Circle It!

Circle the sentence that is true.

Rocks are made up of minerals.

Rocks have the same shape.

Name _____

Word Play

Fill in the blanks. Use each word from the word bank.

rock	pebbles	sand	weathering

The next time you see a big _____,

look closely. Someday the rock may be much smaller!

Wind and rain may wear away at the rock. This is

called _____. Over time, the rock may

break down into small _____. Perhaps

the pebbles will someday break down into tiny pieces

of _____.

You rock!

Apply Concepts

Fill in the chart. Show how rocks can be alike and different.

Rocks

Alike	Different
made of minerals	size

Take It Home!

Family Members: Work with your child to identify objects made from rocks in and around your home.

Ask a Geologist

Now It's Your Turn!

▶ What question would you ask a geologist?

_____

_____

What is a geologist?
A geologist is a scientist who studies Earth. We study the materials on Earth, such as rocks, soil, and water.

How do geologists work?
Some geologists dig up rocks. They work outside with hiking shoes and picks. Others stay in a lab. They use machines to collect and study data about Earth.

How does your work help people?
Geologists find water, oil, and gas underground. These are resources people need. We also study earthquakes and volcanoes to help people stay safe.

Tools of the Trade

▶ Explore what geologists do. How do you think each tool helps a geologist? Write your answers.

helmet

pick

compass

Essential Question

What Are Sources of Water?

Engage Your Brain!

Find the answer to the question in the lesson.

Which source of water is both fresh and frozen?

_____

Active Reading

Lesson Vocabulary

1 Preview the lesson.

2 Write the 3 vocabulary terms here.

_____ _____

_____ _____

© Houghton Mifflin Harcourt Publishing Company (c) © Fotolia

Water, Water, Everywhere

Water is an important natural resource. It is found many places on Earth. Water is on Earth's surface, underground, and in the air. Oceans hold most of Earth's water. Water is also in rivers, lakes, and glaciers.

Active Reading

A detail is a fact about a main idea. Draw one line under a detail. Draw an arrow to the main idea it tells about.

Water is underground. It may flow in spaces between rocks underground. It may form pools underground.

Water is in the air. You can see it in the form of clouds.

▶ **Where can water be found on Earth? Name two places.**

glaciers waterfall

It's Fresh

Fresh water is water with very little salt. Most living things need fresh water to live.

There are many natural sources of fresh water. It is in glaciers, rivers, ponds, and most lakes.

A **glacier** is a large, thick sheet of slow-moving ice. It is made of frozen fresh water. Glaciers hold most of Earth's fresh water.

A lake is a large body of water with land all around it. The water in a lake does not flow. Most lakes are fresh water. A pond is a very small lake.

A river is a large body of flowing fresh water. Rivers flow into larger bodies of water, such as oceans.

▶ Read the captions. Identify the properties of sources of fresh water. Circle two properties of a glacier. Underline two properties of a lake. Draw two lines under two properties of a river.

183

Salt of the Earth

Most water on Earth is salt water.
Salt water is water that has much more salt than fresh water. Salt water is found mostly in oceans and seas.

Active Reading

The main idea is the most important idea about something. Draw two lines under the main idea.

The Great Salt Lake in Utah is a salt water lake. There are very few salt water lakes on Earth.

A sea is a large body of salt water. It usually has land on most of its sides.

An ocean is a very large body of salt water. It is larger than a sea. Most of Earth's water is in oceans. Oceans cover most of Earth's surface.

▶ Read the captions. Identify the properties of sources of salt water. Circle two properties of a sea. Underline two properties of an ocean.

Sum It Up!

1 Mark It!

Which natural source of water is salt water?
Mark it with an X to identify it.

2 Write It!

Compare these natural sources of water.
Tell what you know about each one.

Fresh   Salt   Fresh

Name _____

Word Play

Read each word. Draw lines through the maze to connect each word to its definition.

| lake | river | ocean | glacier |

| very large body of salt water | flowing body of fresh water | sheet of frozen fresh water | water with land all around it |

Apply Concepts

Write about the properties of each natural source of water. Include whether it is fresh water or salt water.

Sources of Water

Lakes	Oceans	Rivers	Glaciers
_____	_____	_____	_____
_____	_____	_____	_____
_____	_____	_____	_____
_____	_____	_____	_____
_____	_____	_____	_____
_____	_____	_____	_____
_____	_____	_____	_____
_____	_____	_____	_____

Take It Home!

Family Members: Have your child find pictures from books or online to identify natural sources of water. Have him or her describe the properties of each source, including whether it is fresh water or salt water.

TEKS **2.1C** identify and demonstrate how to use, conserve, and dispose of natural resources and materials such as conserving water and reuse or recycling of paper, plastic, and metal
2.7C distinguish between natural and manmade resources

Essential Question

What Are Resources?

🧠 Engage Your Brain!

Find the answer to the question in the lesson.

Look at the statues. What natural resource are they made from?

They are made from _____.

Active Reading

Lesson Vocabulary

❶ Preview the lesson.

❷ Write the 2 vocabulary terms here.

_____ _____

It's Natural!

A **natural resource** is anything from nature that people can use. Some important natural resources are rocks, soil, water, and air.

Active Reading

Find the sentence that tells the meaning of **natural resource**. Draw a line under the sentence.

People use rocks to make buildings, roads, and walls.

People use soil to grow plants. Soil has nutrients and water that plants need to grow.

People breathe air to live.

People drink water. They also use it to cook, bathe, and clean.

▶ Identify how people use natural resources. Draw one way.

It's Second Nature

Animals and plants are important natural resources, too. They come from nature, and people can use them. Look at how people use animals and plants.

Active Reading

The main idea is the most important idea about something. Draw two lines under the main idea.

Some people use animals for food and clothing. They eat eggs from chickens. They use wool from sheep to make warm clothes.

© Houghton Mifflin Harcourt Publishing Company (bg) ©David R. Frazier/Photo Researchers; (t) ©Marty Rekusen/cultura/Corbis

People use plants for food. They also use plants to make and build things. Wood and cotton come from plants.

▶ Identify how people use plants. Draw one way.

People Power

Not all resources can be found in nature. There are some resources that only people can make.

A **human-made resource** is something made by humans for people to use. Some examples are steel, nylon, and plastic.

Steel is a strong material. It is lightweight. Steel lasts a long time.

Nylon is a strong material, but it is easy to stretch. It is hard to tear nylon.

Plastic is easy to make. It can be formed into many shapes.

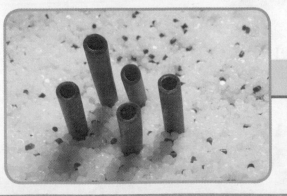

► Identify how people use materials. Draw one thing people make from plastic.

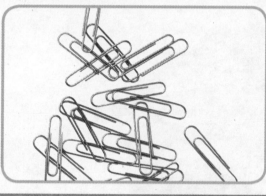

Things like paper clips and tools are made from steel.

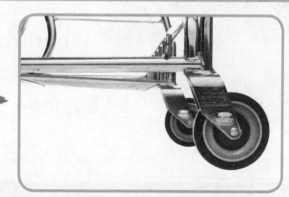

Things like small wheels and clothes are made from nylon.

Things like lunchboxes and bottles are made from plastic.

Where Does It Come From?

Can you tell if the resource is natural or human-made? Circle a label to show your answer.

rocks

natural

human-made

nylon

natural

human-made

plastic

natural

human-made

steel

natural

human-made

soil

natural

human-made

vegetable

natural

human-made

Sum It Up!

① Write It!

Identify two ways you use water.

_____

_____

_____

② Draw It!

Draw one way you used a natural resource today.

③ Mark It!

Circle the resources that are human-made. Place an X over the resources that are natural.

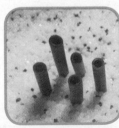  

Name _____

Word Play

Write the definitions.

natural resource: human-made resource:

_____   _____

_____   _____

_____   _____

Match each object to the resource it is made from. Is the resource natural or human-made?

_____

_____

Apply Concepts

Which resources are natural? Which resources are human-made? Use the words in the word bank to complete the chart.

| eggs | soil | rocks | nylon | air | plastic |
| vegetables | steel | water | | | |

Resources

Natural	Human-made
_____	_____
_____	_____
_____	_____
_____	_____
_____	_____
_____	_____

Take It Home!

Family Members: Walk around your house with your child. Ask him or her to identify resources and distinguish them as natural or human-made. Talk about how you use those resources.

TEKS 2.2A ask questions about organisms, objects, and events during observations and investigations **2.2B** plan and conduct descriptive investigations such as how organisms grow **2.2D** record and organize data using pictures, numbers, and words

Name _____

Essential Question

How Can We Classify Plant Products?

Set a Purpose

Tell what you will do.

_____

_____

Think About the Procedure

❶ How will you know which products belong in the same group?

_____

_____

❷ How will you record the groups you made?

_____

_____

Record Your Data

Record and organize your data in this chart. Write a name for each group. Then write the products in each group.

Group 1	Group 2	Group 3
_____	_____	_____

Draw Conclusions

What are some kinds of products that people make from plants?

_____

_____

Ask More Questions

What other questions can you ask about plant products?

_____

_____

Picture Cards

Cut the cards along the dashed lines.

peanut butter

cotton shirt

wood table

straw hat

grape jelly

seagrass slippers

cotton blankets

maple syrup

corn cereal

TEKS **2.3A** identify and explain a problem in his/her own words and propose a task and solution for the problem such as lack of water in a habitat

Engineering and Technology

How It's Made
Cotton Shirt

A cotton shirt is made from cotton plants. It takes many steps to make cotton into a shirt.

Raw cotton is picked and cleaned.

The cotton is spun into thread. The thread is woven into fabric.

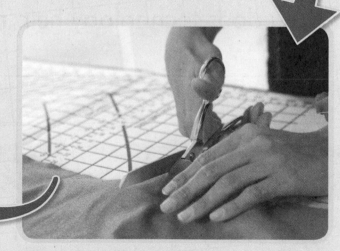

The fabric is cut into pieces. The pieces are sewn together.

Out of Order

Write 1 to 4 to show the correct order of steps for making a cotton shirt. The first step is 1.

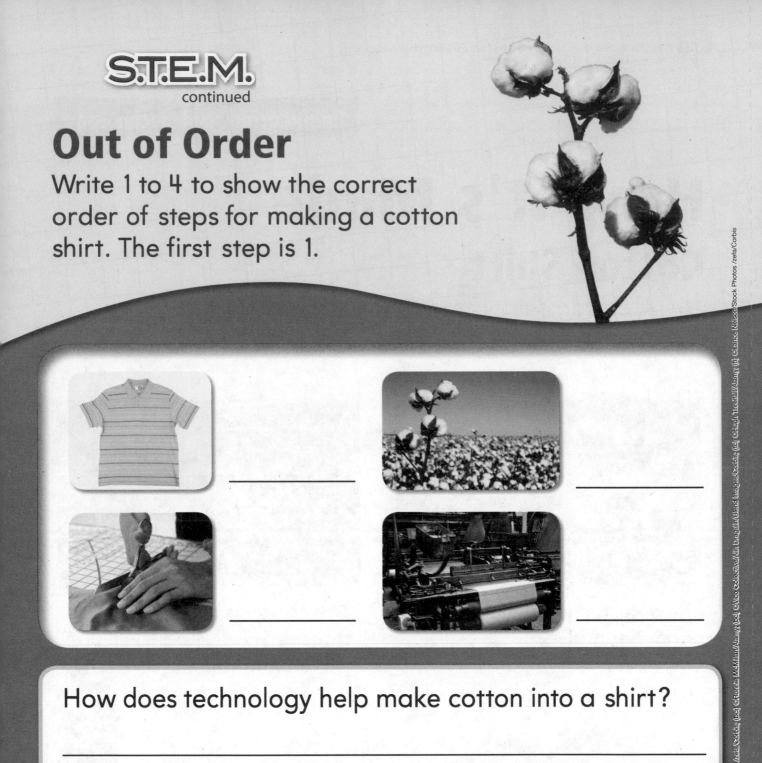

How does technology help make cotton into a shirt?

_____

_____

Build On It!

Test your ideas about building safety. Complete **Test It: Strong Buildings** on the Inquiry Flipchart.

TEKS 2.1C identify and demonstrate how to use, conserve, and dispose of natural resources and materials such as conserving water and reuse or recycling of paper, plastic, and metal

Lesson **5**

Essential Question

How Can We Save Resources?

Engage Your Brain!

Find the answer to the question in the lesson.

Look at the art project. How are materials being conserved?

They are being

_____ .

Active Reading

Lesson Vocabulary

① Preview the lesson.

② Write the 5 vocabulary terms here.

_____   _____

_____   _____

Conserve It!

We use natural resources and materials every day. In time, natural resources and materials will be used up. We must conserve them. **Conserve** means to use things wisely to make them last longer. Look at the pictures to see how you can conserve natural resources and materials.

Active Reading

Find the sentence that tells the meaning of **conserve**. Draw a line under the sentence.

Turn off the water when you brush your teeth. This conserves water. Water is a natural resource.

Turn off the lights when you leave a room. This conserves electricity. Electricity comes from natural resources.

Shop with reusable bags. This conserves materials like paper and plastic.

▶ Read the captions. Identify a way to conserve natural resources. Circle it. Identify a way to conserve materials. Draw a box around it.

The Three Rs

You can reuse, reduce, and recycle to conserve natural resources and materials.

Reuse

Reuse means to use again. When you reuse things, you make less trash. You also need fewer new things made from natural resources. You can reuse a metal can as a lantern.

Reduce

Reduce means to use less. This boy uses a refillable bottle to drink water from his refrigerator. This reduces the number of plastic bottles he uses.

Recycle

Glass, paper, metal, and plastic can be recycled. **Recycle** means to use the materials in old things to make new things. This makes less trash. Old paper can be recycled into new paper.

▶ Identify a way you can conserve a material around your home.

_____

_____

All's Well That Ends Well

Suppose you finish using a bottle or napkin. What should you do with it? After you use resources and materials, you must dispose of them. **Dispose** means to get rid of something.

Active Reading

The main idea is the most important idea about something. Draw two lines under the main idea.

How can you reuse materials?

Think before you dispose! Can you use a resource or material again? Can you recycle it? Can you compost it? Composting means adding food scraps to soil. This makes the soil rich.

Not everything can be reused or recycled. Sometimes you must throw away trash. Put trash in trashcans. Never litter.

composting

PLEASE DO NOT LITTER

putting trash in trashcans

▶ Identify a way to dispose of a natural resource.

_____

▶ Identify a way to dispose of a material.

_____

Sum It Up!

① Write It!

Identify two ways you can conserve natural resources and materials.

_____

_____

_____

② Match It!

Identify how to dispose of these materials. Draw lines to match.

③ Draw It!

How could you reuse this can? Draw one way.

Name _____

Word Play

Read the clues. Use the words to complete the puzzle.

| conserve | dispose | recycle | reduce | reuse |

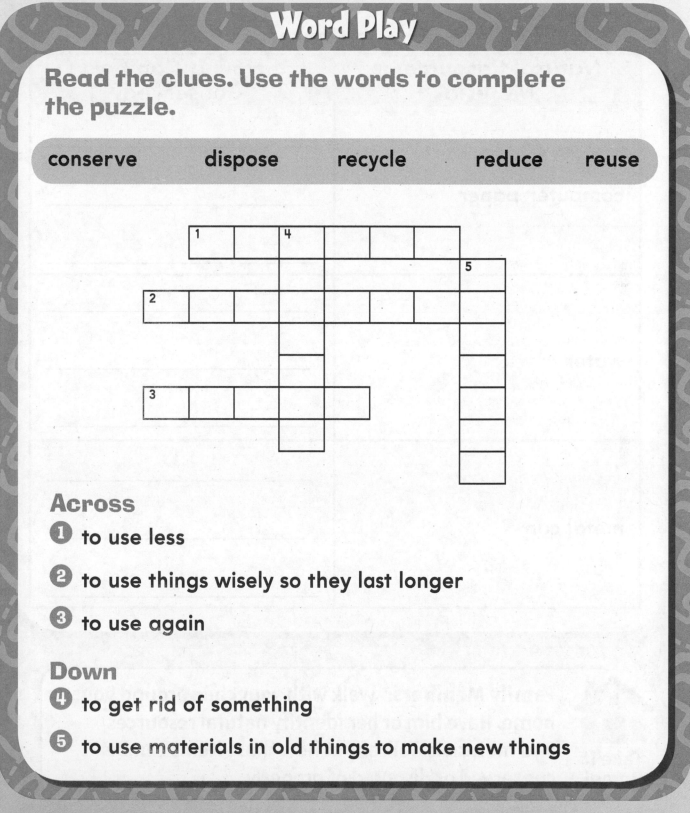

Across

1 to use less

2 to use things wisely so they last longer

3 to use again

Down

4 to get rid of something

5 to use materials in old things to make new things

Apply Concepts

How can each natural resource or material be conserved? Fill in the chart.

How to Conserve

Natural Resource or Material	How It Can Be Conserved
computer paper	_____ _____ _____
water	_____ _____ _____
metal can	_____ _____ _____

Take It Home!

Family Members: Walk with your child around your home. Have him or her identify natural resources and materials. Talk about how those items can be conserved or disposed of properly.

Name _____

Vocabulary Review

Use the terms in the box to complete the sentences.

> fresh water
> recycle
> rock

TEKS 2.1C

1. You _____ when you use the materials in old things to make new things.

TEKS 2.7A

2. A _____ is a hard, nonliving object from the ground.

TEKS 2.7B

3. Water with very little salt is _____.

Science Concepts

Fill in the letter of the choice that best answers the question.

TEKS 2.7A

4. Which is smallest?

Ⓐ a boulder

Ⓑ a pebble

Ⓒ a piece of sand

TEKS 2.7C

5. What are natural resources?

Ⓐ things people cannot live without

Ⓑ things people make to protect nature

Ⓒ things from nature that people can use

TEKS 2.7B

6. Which sentence best describes the properties of this body of water?

Ⓐ It is fresh water.

Ⓑ It is salt water.

Ⓒ It can be either fresh water or salt water.

TEKS 2.7C

7. Which of these resources is human-made?

Ⓐ eggs

Ⓑ soil

Ⓒ steel

TEKS 2.7A

8. How are these rocks sorted?

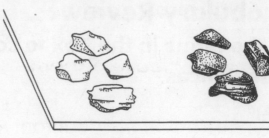

Ⓐ by color

Ⓑ by shape

Ⓒ by size

TEKS 2.1C

9. How can Vindra best conserve natural resources?

Ⓐ She can dispose of trash in trash cans.

Ⓑ She can ask others not to litter.

Ⓒ She can turn off the water when brushing her teeth.

TEKS 2.1C

10. Which is an example of how you can reuse a material?

Ⓐ I can turn off the lights when I leave a room.

Ⓑ I can make a planter out of an egg carton.

Ⓒ I can put old newspapers in a recycling bin.

TEKS 2.7B

11. Compare these natural sources of fresh water. Which source flows?

Ⓐ a river

Ⓑ a pond

Ⓒ a lake

TEKS 2.1C

12. Look at this natural resource.

How can people use this resource?

Ⓐ to cook

Ⓑ to grow plants

Ⓒ to make buildings

Inquiry and the Big Idea
Write the answers to these questions.

TEKS 2.7B

13. a. Identify the properties of an ocean and a sea.

_____

_____

b. How are they the same? How are they different?

_____

_____

TEKS 2.1C

14. a. Why is it important to conserve natural resources and materials?

_____

_____

b. Identify a way to conserve natural resources.

_____

c. Identify a way to dispose of materials.

_____

All About Weather

tornado

> **Big Idea**
>
> There are patterns in weather and the seasons. The seasons affect living things.

TEKS 2.2A, 2.2B, 2.2C, 2.2D, 2.2E, 2.2F, 2.4A, 2.8A, 2.8B, 2.8C, 2.9B

I Wonder Why

People keep extra food and other supplies in case of a storm. Why?

Turn the page to find out.

Here's Why People keep extra supplies in case the power goes out and the stores are closed.

In this unit, you will explore this Big Idea, the Essential Questions, and the Investigations on the Inquiry Flipchart.

Levels of Inquiry Key ■ DIRECTED ■ GUIDED ■ INDEPENDENT

Track Your Progress

Big Idea There are patterns in weather and the seasons. The seasons affect living things.

Essential Questions

Now I Get the Big Idea!

Science Notebook

Before you begin each lesson, be sure to write your thoughts about the Essential Question.

TEKS 2.4A collect, record, and compare information using tools, including . . . weather instruments such as thermometers, wind vanes, and rain gauges . . . 2.8A measure, record, and graph weather information, including temperature, wind conditions, precipitation, and cloud coverage, in order to identify patterns in the data

Essential Question

How Does Weather Change?

Engage Your Brain!

Find the answer to the question in the lesson.

What kind of weather do these clouds bring?

_____

Active Reading

Lesson Vocabulary

1 Preview the lesson.

2 Write the 4 vocabulary terms here.

_____   _____

_____   _____

Wonderful Weather

Weather is what the air outside is like. Weather may be sunny, rainy, cloudy, snowy, or windy. It can be hot or cold outside. Weather can change quickly, or it can change over many days or months.

Active Reading

The main idea is the most important idea about something. Draw a line under the main idea on this page.

Some days are warm and sunny.

On some days, rain falls.

► Draw what the weather is like today.

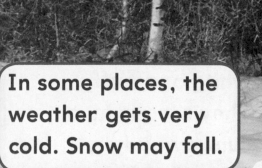

In some places, the weather gets very cold. Snow may fall.

225

Send In the Clouds

A cloud is a group of tiny drops of water or ice crystals. The drops are so light that they float in the air. The water drops may get bigger and heavier. When the drops get too heavy to float, they fall as rain or snow.

Clouds are clues about how the weather may change.

Active Reading

An effect tells what happens. What happens when water drops get too heavy? Draw two lines under the effect.

Cumulus clouds are white and puffy. They usually mean sunny weather.

Stratus clouds are gray and flat. They often cover the sky. Stratus clouds may bring rain or snow.

Observe the weather where you live. Record and describe the kind of clouds you see.

Stratus

Cirrus clouds are high in the sky. These thin, wispy clouds usually mean sunny weather.

Cumulonimbus clouds are thunderstorm clouds. These clouds are tall and puffy.

227

Measure It!

You can use tools to measure weather.

A rain gauge measures precipitation.

Precipitation is water that falls from the sky.

Rain, snow, sleet, and hail are precipitation.

A thermometer measures temperature.

Temperature is how hot or cold something is.

Active Reading

Find the sentence that tells the meaning of **precipitation**. Draw a line under the sentence.

Air is all around us. Wind is moving air that surrounds us and takes up space. A weather vane tells the direction of the wind.

This thermometer measures temperature in degrees Fahrenheit and Celsius.

A rain gauge tells how much rain falls.

Do the Math!
Measure Temperature

Use a thermometer to measure the temperature of the air in the morning and in the afternoon. Color the pictures below to record and compare the temperatures. Write the temperatures on the lines.

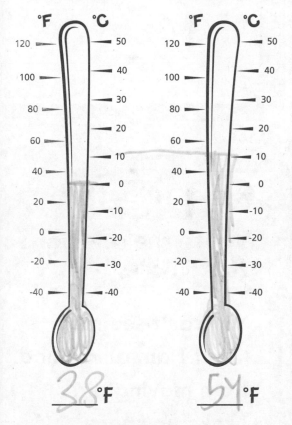

Morning **Afternoon**

38 °F   54 °F

Write a subtraction sentence to find out how the temperature changed.

Sum It Up!

① Draw It!

Draw your favorite kind of weather.

② Match It!

Match each tool to what it measures.

temperature

rain

③ Solve It!

Write the answer to this riddle.

You can't see me,
    but I am all around.
I am moving air.
I take up space.
    What am I?

_____

④ Order It!

Write 1, 2, 3 to order these thermometers from hottest to coldest. Use 1 for the hottest.

_____   _____   _____

Name _____

Word Play

Read the clues. Use the words to complete the puzzle.

| weather | temperature | precipitation | wind |

Across

1 What the air outside is like

2 Moving air that surrounds you and takes up space

Down

3 Water that falls as rain, snow, sleet, or hail

4 How hot or cold something is

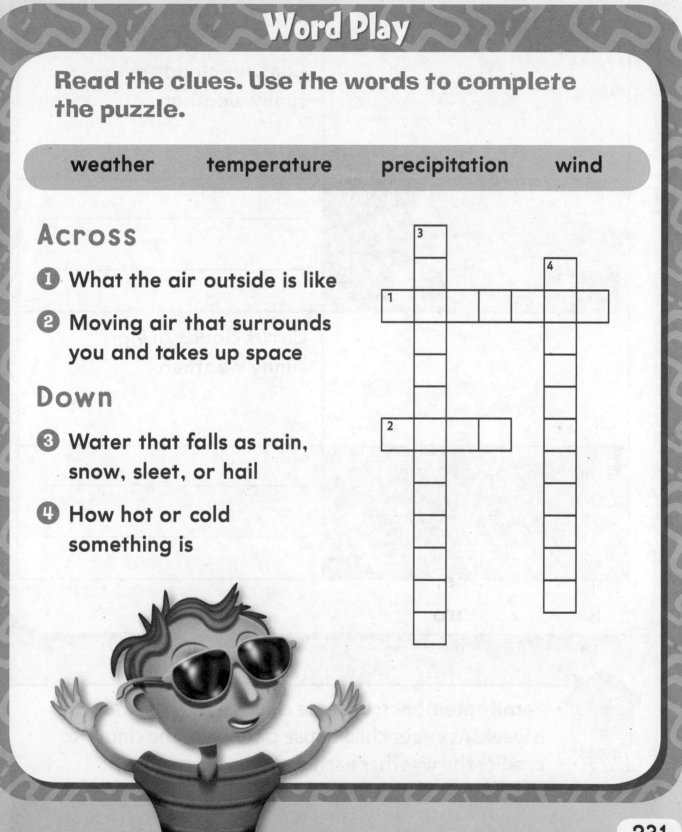

Apply Concepts

Write and draw to complete the chart.

Clouds and Weather

Clouds	Weather
	Cumulus clouds mean sunny weather.
	_____ _____
	Cirrus clouds bring sunny weather.
	_____ _____

© Houghton Mifflin Harcourt Publishing Company   (t) ©Corbis; (b) ©Getty Images/PhotoDisc

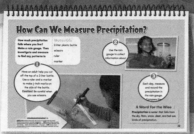

Inquiry Flipchart p. 32

Name _____

Essential Question

How Can We Measure Precipitation?

TEKS **2.2A** ask questions about organisms, objects, and events during observations and investigations **2.2B** plan and conduct descriptive investigations such as how organisms grow **2.2D** record and organize data using pictures, numbers, and words **2.2E** communicate observations and justify explanations using student-generated data from simple descriptive investigations **2.2F** compare results of investigations with what students and scientists know about the world **2.4A** collect, record, and compare information using tools, including . . . weather instruments such as . . . rain gauges **2.8A** measure, record, and graph weather information, including temperature, wind conditions, precipitation, and cloud coverage, in order to identify patterns in the data

Set a Purpose

Tell what you want to find out.

_____

Think About the Procedure

❶ Why do you make marks on the bottle?

_____

_____

❷ Why do you measure each day for two weeks?

_____

_____

_____

Record Your Data

In each box, write the day's precipitation in inches and **R** for rain, **SN** for snow, **SL** for sleet, and **H** for hail.

	Day 1	Day 2	Day 3	Day 4	Day 5	Day 6	Day 7
Week 1							
Week 2							

Draw Conclusions

On which day did the most precipitation fall? Use your data to tell how you know.

_____

_____

Scientists measure weather to see patterns. Compare your results with what scientists know. Did you see any weather patterns? Explain.

_____

_____

Ask More Questions

What other questions could you ask about measuring weather?

_____

_____

TEKS **2.8A** measure, record, and graph weather information, including temperature, wind conditions, precipitation, and cloud coverage, in order to identify patterns in the data **2.8C** explore the processes in the water cycle, including evaporation, condensation, and precipitation, as connected to weather conditions

Essential Question

What Are Some Weather Patterns?

Engage Your Brain!

Find the answer to the question in the lesson.

What is the scientist doing?

The scientist is

_____ .

Active Reading

Lesson Vocabulary

1. Preview the lesson.

2. Write the 4 vocabulary terms here.

_____   _____

_____   _____

A Perfect Pattern

Weather can change from hour to hour and from day to day. It changes in a pattern. A **weather pattern** is a weather change that repeats over and over.

Active Reading

Find the sentence that tells the meaning of **weather pattern**. Draw a line under the sentence.

Gentle Morning

The sun is low in the sky. It is just starting to warm Earth. The air is still cool.

Afternoon So Bright

The sun is high in the sky. It has warmed Earth and the air.

236

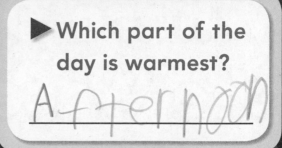

▶ Which part of the day is warmest?

Afternoon

Evening Shade

The sun is setting. It does not warm Earth as much. The air is cooling.

Night Fall

We cannot see the sun. The air is cooler. Tomorrow the pattern will begin again.

Where Does the Water Go?

The **water cycle** is the way water moves from Earth's surface into the air and back again. The water cycle is another pattern. The water cycle causes weather to change. Explore the steps of the water cycle.

The sun's heat makes water **evaporate**, or change to a gas. The gas is pushed up and meets cooler air.

Then the gas cools and condenses, or changes into tiny drops of water. The drops form clouds.

The water drops join to make bigger ones. The drops fall as precipitation.

The precipitation flows into rivers, lakes, and oceans. Then the water cycle starts again.

▶ How are condensation and precipitation connected to weather?

_____

_____

_____

Weather Watch

How do you know what to wear when you go outside? You think about the weather. Knowing about the weather helps people plan activities. It helps them stay safe, too.

Scientists help people find out more about weather. Scientists use tools to measure weather. Measuring weather helps scientists see patterns. Patterns help scientists predict weather. Then they can tell people what kind of weather is coming.

This weather tool measures temperature, wind speed, and precipitation.

▶ How do you think this weather tool helps people stay safe?

_____

_____

You can track and record weather data at home and at school. Over time, the data show patterns.

	Monday	Tuesday	Wednesday	Thursday	Friday
	☀	☁	🌧	🌤	☀
High	76	73	73	77	
Low	58	57	57	62	

▶ A weather report says that the day will be rainy and cold. Draw the clothes you would wear.

Sum It Up!

① Match It!

Match each picture to the word that tells about it.

morning

afternoon

② Answer It!

Fill in the blank.

What is the movement of water from Earth's surface into the air and back again called?

_____

③ Write It!

Write two reasons it is important to track weather.

_____

_____

_____

Name _____

Word Play

Fill in the blanks with words from the box.

| measure | evaporate | condense | water |

( )__ __ __ __ moves in a cycle.
1

Heat can cause water to change to a gas, or

___ ___( )___ ___ ___ ___( )___.
2   3

Scientists use tools to ___ ___( )___ ___ ___ ___ weather.
4

Water can ___ ___ ___ ___( )( )___ ___ into drops.
5 6

Use the circled letters to write the answer to the question.

What do you call a weather change that repeats over and over?

a ___ e ___ ___ her p ___ t t ___ r ___
1   2   3   4   5   6

Apply Concepts

Fill in the chart. Show how the steps of the water cycle are connected to weather.

Water Cycle

Cause		Effect

| The sun heats water on Earth's surface. | ➤ | _____ _____ _____ |

| Water condenses into drops. | ➤ | _____ _____ _____ |

| _____ _____ _____ | ➤ | The drops fall to Earth as precipitation. |

TEKS **2.2A** ask questions about organisms, objects, and events during observations and investigations **2.2B** plan and conduct descriptive investigations . . . **2.2C** collect data from observations using simple equipment . . . **2.2D** record and organize data using . . . numbers **2.2E** communicate observations and justify explanations using student-generated data from simple descriptive investigations **2.2F** compare results of investigations with what students and scientists know about the world **2.8C** explore the processes in the water cycle, including evaporation, condensation, and precipitation, as connected to weather conditions

Name _____

Essential Question

What Is Evaporation?

Set a Purpose

Write what you want to find out.

Does water evaporate the same in an open and close

State Your Hypothesis

Write your hypothesis, or the statement that you will test.

I think the one with No Lide will have Lest.

Think About the Procedure

1 Why should both containers start with the same amount of water?

To make it fair.

2 Why does one container have a lid?

To see what hapens.

_____

Record Your Data

Use your data to communicate your observations.

	How much water?	
	Before	After
Container with a Lid	4cm	4cm
Container with no Lid	4cm	3½cm

Draw Conclusions

Compare your results with your hypothesis. What happened to the water in the open container? What is evaporation? How is evaporation connected to weather and the water cycle?

The water evaporated and went into the air.

Ask More Questions

What other questions can you ask about evaporation?

TEKS **2.8B** identify the importance of weather and seasonal information to make choices in clothing, activities, and transportation **2.9B** identify factors in the environment, including temperature and precipitation, that affect growth and behavior such as migration, hibernation, and dormancy of living things

Essential Question

How Do Seasons Affect Living Things?

Engage Your Brain!

Find the answer to the question in the lesson.

When might you see ice on plants?

You might see this in _Winter_ .

Active Reading

Lesson Vocabulary

1. Preview the lesson.

2. Write the 4 vocabulary terms here.

_____   _____

_____   _____

© Houghton Mifflin Harcourt Publishing Company (bg) ©Mauritius GmbH/Alamy

Season to Season

A **season** is a time of year that has a certain kind of weather. Weather changes each season. The seasons follow the same pattern every year.

Fabulous Fall

In fall the air outside may be cool. Leaves of some trees change color and drop off.

Wonderful Winter

Winter is the coldest season. Ice can form on land and plants. In some places snow may fall. Winter has the fewest hours of daylight.

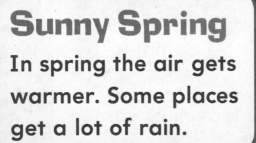
Sunny Spring

In spring the air gets warmer. Some places get a lot of rain.

Super Summer

Summer is the warmest season. Some places have sudden storms. Summer has the most hours of daylight.

A Change of Pace

Changes in temperature, sunlight, and precipitation from season to season affect many living things.

▶ How does rainfall affect how plants grow? How does temperature affect how plants grow?

_____

_____

fall

winter

spring

summer

There is cooler weather in fall. The leaves of some plants change color and drop off. By winter, the plants have lost their leaves. In spring, more rain and warmer weather cause new leaves to grow. Leaves keep growing in summer.

Less sunlight and cooler temperatures cause plants to lose their leaves. The plants stop growing and go through dormancy. Dormancy is a time when plants stop growing. Most plants go through dormancy in winter.

dormant tree

Cold temperatures affect animals in winter. Some animals hibernate. To hibernate is to go into a deep, sleeplike state. This helps animals, like bats, save energy when it is cold.

bat hibernating

Animals may migrate during some seasons. To migrate is to travel from one place to another and back again. Watering holes may dry up if there is no rainfall in a season. Some animals will migrate to a place where they can find water.

wildebeest at a watering hole

The Seasons and You

Do you wear a coat on a hot summer day? Do you swim at the beach in winter? Probably not! The seasons affect people, too. The seasons affect what we wear, how we travel, and what we do for fun.

Active Reading

The main idea is the most important idea about something. Draw two lines under the main idea.

The seasons affect the clothes you wear. You may wear cooler clothes in spring. You may wear warmer clothes in fall.

The seasons may affect how you travel. You may ride in a car or a bus in winter. You may ride your bike in summer.

The seasons affect what activities you can do.

▶ Identify an activity you could do on a hot, summer day.

run outside.

Sum It Up!

① Match It!

Match the picture to the word that tells about it.

spring

winter

② Circle It!

Circle the ways a tree can change with the seasons.

Its leaves drop off.

It migrates.

Its leaves change color.

③ Write It!

It is a cold, snowy day where you live. Identify the kind of clothing you would wear outside.

_____

_____

_____

④ Answer It!

A gray whale swims from cold waters to warm waters in winter. What is this an example of?

_____

Word Play

Name _____

Fill in the blanks. Use each word from the word bank.

| hibernate | fall | season | migrate |

Dear Aunt Lucy,

Thanks for letting me come see you. Summer is usually my favorite _____ to visit you. This time, I liked being there in _____ when the leaves were changing color.

Walking in the woods was great. It was the first time I saw birds starting to _____ to their winter homes. It was cool to learn that gophers _____. I'll have to come in spring when they wake up!

Your nephew,

Ben

Apply Concepts

Fill in the chart. Show how seasons affect living things.

How Seasons Affect Living Things

Plants	Animals	People
_____	_____	_____
_____	_____	_____
_____	_____	_____
_____	_____	_____
_____	_____	_____
_____	_____	_____
_____	_____	_____
_____	_____	_____

Take It Home!

Family Members: Ask your child to choose a favorite season. Then discuss how changes in that season affect living things such as plants, animals, and people.

TEKS 2.3A identify and explain a problem in his/her own words and propose a task and solution for the problem, such as lack of water in a habitat 2.4A collect, record, and compare information using tools, including...weather instruments such as thermometers, wind vanes, and rain gauges...

Watching Weather

Hurricane Airplanes

Hurricane airplanes collect data about hurricanes. The data help scientists predict and track hurricanes.

The airplane flies close to a hurricane.

Weather tools are placed in tubes. The plane drops the tubes into the hurricane.

The tubes fall into the center of the hurricane. The tools in the tubes collect storm data.

Weather Technology

Look at the diagram of the weather tube. Then answer the questions.

The parachute slows down the tube as it falls through the hurricane.

The tube holds weather tools. The tools collect data about wind speed and temperature.

What might happen if the parachute did not open?

_____

_____

Build On It!

 Make a plan for your own weather station. Complete **Improvise It: Weather Station** on the Inquiry Flipchart.

Ask a Storm Chaser

What kinds of storms do storm chasers look for?
Most storm chasers look for tornadoes. A few storm chasers look for hurricanes.

How do you work?
Storm chasers watch the weather carefully. We learn about bad storms. We try to predict where to find them. Then we drive to see a storm.

How does storm chasing help other people?
Most storm chasers work with weather centers. If we spot a storm, we can alert the police and people on farms.

Now It's Your Turn!

▶ What question would you ask a storm chaser?

_____

_____

Safety from the Storm

▶ Draw or write the answer to each question to get to safety.

1 Your family has a storm kit. You use it if you lose power or get hurt. Draw one thing you would put in a storm kit.

2 A storm might be coming. Why should you make a plan?

3 Storm chasers spot a tornado. Draw a picture of what they might see.

4 Tornado warning! Your family follows its safety plan by finding shelter. Why?

1

2
_____

_____

_____

3

4
_____

_____

_____

Name _____

Vocabulary Review

Use the terms in the box to complete the sentences.

> hibernate
> precipitation
> weather
> pattern

TEKS 2.8C

1. Water that falls from the sky is

   _____.

TEKS 2.8A

2. A weather change that repeats over and over is

   a _____.

TEKS 2.9B

3. When animals go into a deep, sleeplike state in winter, they _____.

Science Concepts

Fill in the letter of the choice that best answers the question.

TEKS 2.8B

4. In which season are you **most likely** to wear a coat and mittens?

   Ⓐ spring

   Ⓑ summer

   Ⓒ winter

TEKS 2.4A, 2.8A

5. You want to observe and measure how much it rains each day for two weeks. Which tool should you use?

   Ⓐ a rain gauge

   Ⓑ a thermometer

   Ⓒ a weather vane

Use this picture of the water cycle to answer questions 6 and 7.

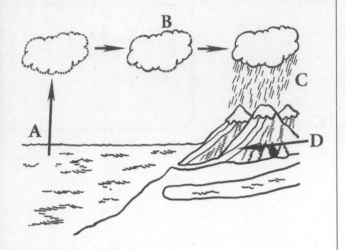

TEKS 2.8C

6. Which step shows evaporation?

Ⓐ Step A

Ⓑ Step B

Ⓒ Step C

TEKS 2.8C

7. What is happening in Step C?

Ⓐ condensation

Ⓑ evaporation

Ⓒ precipitation

TEKS 2.8C

8. Oscar sets up this experiment with an open container of water.

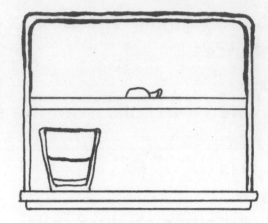

What will he probably observe the next day?

Ⓐ There will be less water in the container.

Ⓑ There will be the same amount of water in the container.

Ⓒ There will be more water in the container.

TEKS 2.8B

9. Ella sees that it is very windy and rainy outside. Which is the safest way for Ella to get to school?

Ⓐ walking

Ⓑ riding a bike

Ⓒ riding a bus

TEKS 2.9B

10. Some animals hibernate to save energy. When do they hibernate?

Ⓐ when the weather is hot

Ⓑ when the weather is cold

Ⓒ when the weather is dry

TEKS 2.4A, 2.8A

11. What do you measure with this tool?

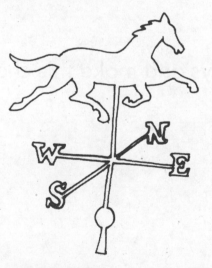

Ⓐ the direction of the wind

Ⓑ rainfall

Ⓒ temperature

Use this chart to answer questions 12 and 13.

Month	Average Temperature	Total Rainfall
January	26 °F	2.5 in.
April	52 °F	3.6 in.
July	75 °F	4.4 in.
October	54 °F	2.7 in.

TEKS 2.2D, 2.8A

12. In which two months was the average temperature about the same?

Ⓐ January and July

Ⓑ July and October

Ⓒ April and October

TEKS 2.2D, 2.8A

13. When did it rain the most?

Ⓐ April

Ⓑ July

Ⓒ October

Inquiry and the Big Idea

Write the answers to these questions.

TEKS 2.8B, 2.9B

14. a. Why do some animals migrate?

_____

_____

b. How do your choices in clothing and activities change in winter? Name two ways.

_____

_____

TEKS 2.2D, 2.8A, 2.8B

15. You observe the weather for two days and make this chart.

Our Weather				
Monday	Tuesday	Wednesday	Thursday	Friday

a. What can you conclude?

_____

b. Why is it important to track and record the weather?

_____

_____

264 **Unit 6** Unit Review

The Solar System

a planetarium

Big Idea

There are patterns among objects in the sky.

TEKS 2.2A, 2.2B, 2.2D, 2.2E, 2.8D

I Wonder Why

These people are looking at the nighttime sky in a planetarium. Why?
Turn the page to find out.

Here's Why A planetarium shows close-up pictures of faraway objects like stars and other planets.

In this unit, you will explore this Big Idea, the Essential Questions, and the Investigations on the Inquiry Flipchart.

Levels of Inquiry Key ■ DIRECTED ■ GUIDED ■ INDEPENDENT

Track Your Progress

Big Idea There are patterns among objects in the sky.

Essential Questions

Now I Get the Big Idea!

Science Notebook

Before you begin each lesson, be sure to write your thoughts about the Essential Question.

Essential Question

What Are Planets and Stars?

Engage Your Brain!

Find the answer to the question in the lesson.

Name the star that Earth moves around.

_____

Active Reading

Lesson Vocabulary

1 Preview the lesson.

2 Write the 5 vocabulary terms here.

_____   _____

_____   _____

_____

All Systems Go!

We live on Earth. Earth is a planet. A **planet** is a large ball of rock or gas that moves around the sun.

The sun, the planets, and the planets' moons are parts of the **solar system**. There are eight planets in our solar system. Earth is a planet in the solar system.

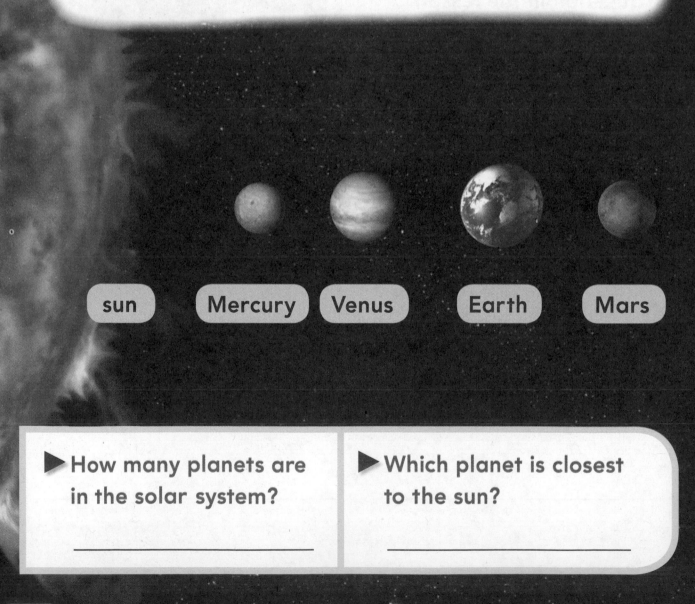

sun   Mercury   Venus   Earth   Mars

▶ How many planets are in the solar system?

_____

▶ Which planet is closest to the sun?

_____

You can see some parts of the solar system only at night. During the day, the parts are still there. You just cannot see them when it is light outside.

Jupiter

Saturn

Uranus

Neptune

The planets look different. They are different sizes. They are different distances from the sun.

The Center of Attention

The sun is the center of the solar system. Earth and the other planets move in orbits around the sun. An **orbit** is the path a planet takes as it moves around the sun.

Planets closer to the sun take less time to make an orbit around the sun. Planets farther away take more time to make an orbit.

Active Reading

The main idea is the most important idea about something. Draw two lines under the main idea.

Venus

Mercury

Mars

sun

It takes one year for Earth to make one orbit around the sun.

Earth

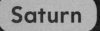
Saturn

Uranus

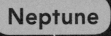
Neptune

▶ Why does Neptune take more time to orbit the sun than Earth takes?

_____

_____

Jupiter

Star Bright

A **star** is a huge ball of hot gases. The hot gases give off light and heat.

The star closest to Earth is the sun. You can see the sun in the daytime, but most stars can be seen only at night. They look like tiny points of light because they are so far away.

Active Reading

Find the sentence that tells the meaning of **star**. Draw a line under the sentence.

The sun gives Earth light and heat.

Some stars form constellations. A **constellation** is a group of stars that forms a pattern. What do these constellations look like to you?

Canis Major

Orion

▶ Why can you see most stars only at night?

_____

_____

273

Sum It Up!

① Solve It!

Write the answer to the riddle.

I am made of planets and a sun.

I have eight planets. Suns, I have only one.

What am I?

_____

② Draw It!

Draw Earth's orbit around the sun.

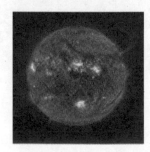

③ Match It!

Match the picture to its description.

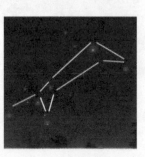

star   planet   constellation

Name _____

Word Play

Write a word from the box for each definition.

| planet | constellation | solar system | orbit |

1 a group of stars that forms a pattern __ __ __ (1) __ __ __ __ __ __ __ __ __ __

2 the path a planet takes as it moves around the sun __ __ __ __ __ (2)

3 a large ball of rock or gas that moves around the sun __ __ __ (3) __ __ __

4 the sun, the planets, and the planets' moons

__ __ __ __ __ __ (4) __ __ __ __ __ __ __ __

Solve the riddle. Write the circled letters in order on the lines below.

I am an object in the sky that gives off light. What am I?

__ __ __ __
1   2   3   4

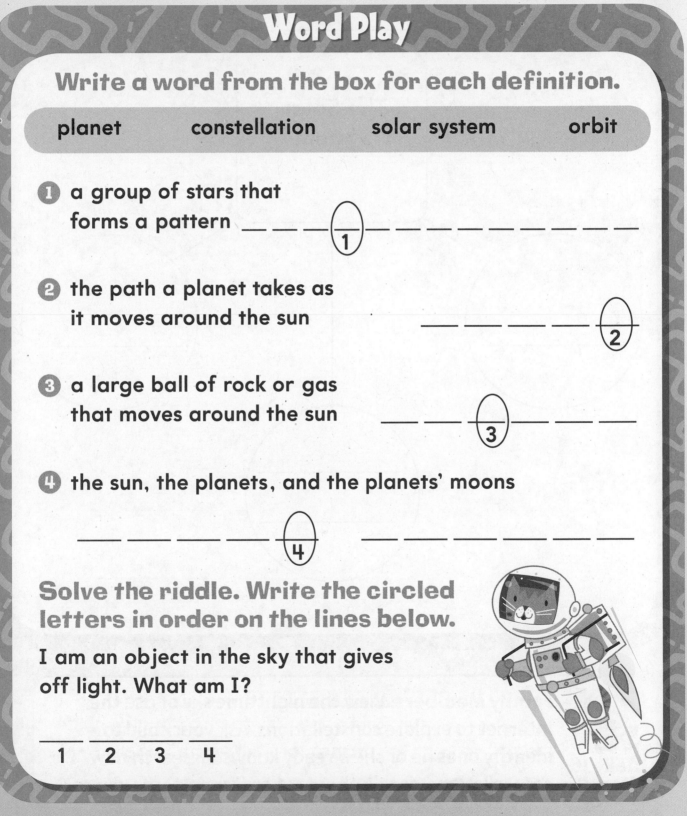

Fill in the chart. Write the parts of the solar system.

The Solar System

_____

_____

_____
_____

Family Members: View the nighttime sky or use the Internet to explore constellations. Ask your child to identify ones he or she already knows. Research new constellations, or talk about other star patterns you see.

Take It Home!

Learn About ...

Annie Jump Cannon

Growing up, Annie Jump Cannon liked to look at stars. She eventually became an astronomer. An astronomer is a scientist who studies stars, planets, and other objects in space.

Cannon studied pictures of stars. The pictures helped her sort stars into groups. Her picture groups were a new way to classify stars. Scientists still classify stars this way today.

Fun Fact

This telescope that Cannon used at the Harvard Observatory was once the largest in the country.

277

Star Power

▶ Explore the work of astronomers.
Write the answer to each question.

1 What does an astronomer study?

2 What are some tools that astronomers use?

3 Why do you think astronomers classify stars?

4 What would you like best about being an astronomer?

1

2

3

4

Essential Question

What Causes Day and Night?

Engage Your Brain!

Find the answer to the question in the lesson.

When it is nighttime in Tokyo, it is morning where you live. Why?

Earth rotates, which causes

_____.

Active Reading

Lesson Vocabulary

1. Preview the lesson.

2. Write the 2 vocabulary terms here.

_____   _____

© Houghton Mifflin Harcourt Publishing Company   (bg) ©B.S.P.I./CORBIS

Turn, Turn, Turn

The sun seems to rise and set each day. Why? The sun does not really move. Earth is moving.

Earth turns. It takes 24 hours for Earth to **rotate**, or make one full turn.

Objects in the sky seem to move in patterns because Earth rotates. Sunrise and sunset take place because Earth rotates.

Active Reading

A cause tells why something happens. Why do objects in the sky seem to move in patterns? Draw one line under the cause.

One rotation, or turn, of Earth takes one day.

Do the Math!

Tell Time

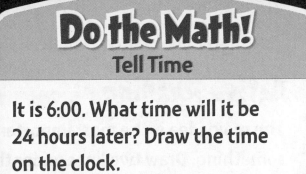

It is 6:00. What time will it be 24 hours later? Draw the time on the clock.

Day and Night

Earth's rotation causes day and night. Look at the pictures. Find the place on Earth that is in sunlight. Observe how day changes to night as Earth rotates.

Active Reading

The main idea is the most important idea about something. Draw two lines under the main idea.

Sunlight shines on the part of Earth facing the sun. This part of Earth has daytime.

day

▶ Mark an X on the part of Earth where it is nighttime.

It is daytime where Earth faces toward the sun. It is nighttime where Earth faces away from the sun. Places on Earth move in and out of the sunlight as Earth rotates. This change causes day and night.

The part of Earth facing away from the sun is dark. This part of Earth has nighttime.

night

▶ Mark an X on the part of Earth where it is daytime.

Cast a Shadow

The sun seems to move across the sky as Earth rotates. Look at the pictures to observe the pattern of the sun. Sunlight shines on objects from different directions as the day goes on. This causes the size, shape, and position of shadows to change.

morning

noon

Shadows are long when the sun is low in the sky. They are shorter when the sun is high in the sky. Look at the pictures to see how a shadow changes.

► Observe the size, shape, and position of the shadows in the pictures. Draw the shadow for early evening.

afternoon

early evening

Over the Moon

The moon orbits, or moves in a path, around Earth. The moon looks different to us as it moves. The **phases** are the shapes of the moon we see as it moves.

It takes about 29 days for the moon to make one orbit around Earth. So the pattern of the phases repeats about every month.

Look at these pictures. Observe the pattern of the phases of the moon.

new moon, day 1

first-quarter moon, day 8

► Describe and record the pattern of the phases of the moon.

_____

_____

_____

_____

full moon, day 15

third-quarter moon, day 22

Sum It Up!

① Circle It!

How long does it takes Earth to rotate one time?

24 minutes

24 hours

24 days

② Write It!

Why does Earth have day and night?

_____

_____

_____

③ Draw It!

Draw to record what each phase of the moon looks like.

new   first quarter   full   third quarter

Name _____

Word Play

Write a word from the word bank to complete each sentence.

| Earth | rotate | phases | shadow | daytime |

1 The part of Earth facing the sun has

_____.

2 It takes 24 hours for Earth to _____ one time.

3 The size, shape, and position of a _____ changes as sunlight shines from different directions.

4 The shapes of the moon you see as it moves are its

_____.

5 There is day and night because _____ rotates.

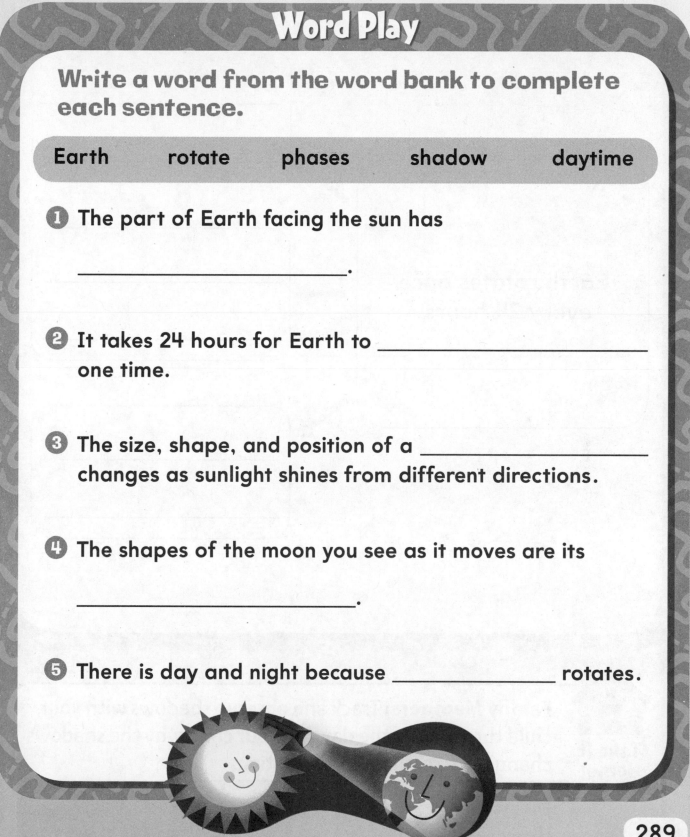

Fill in the chart. Write the effects of Earth's rotation.

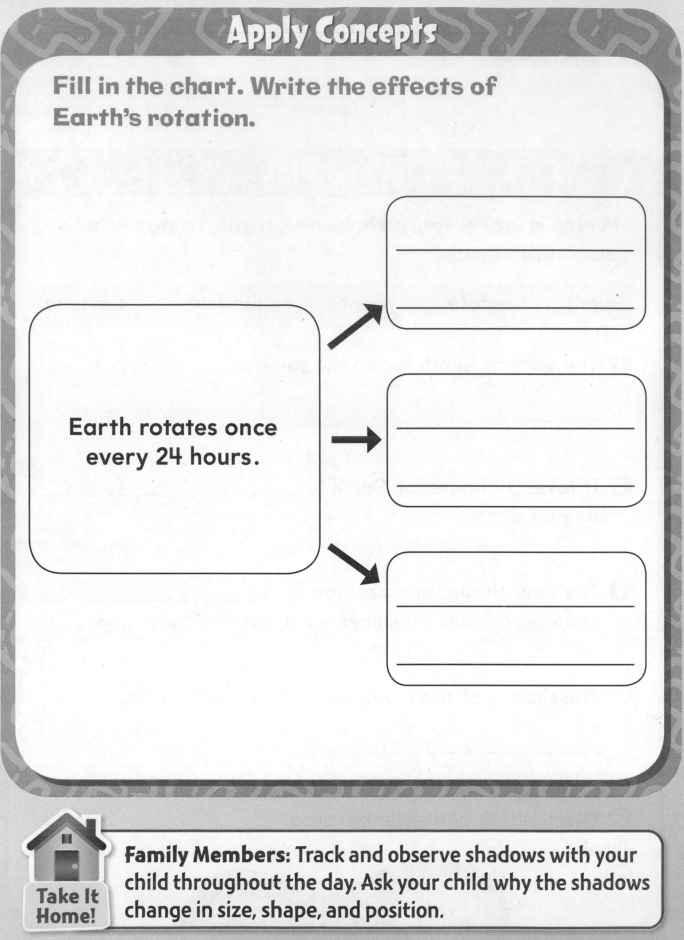

Earth rotates once every 24 hours.

Take It Home!

Family Members: Track and observe shadows with your child throughout the day. Ask your child why the shadows change in size, shape, and position.

290

TEKS 2.3A identify and explain a problem in his/her own words and propose a task and solution for the problem such as lack of water in a habitat

Eye on the Sky
Telescopes

A telescope is a tool that makes faraway objects look larger. It helps people see the details of stars, planets, and other faraway objects.

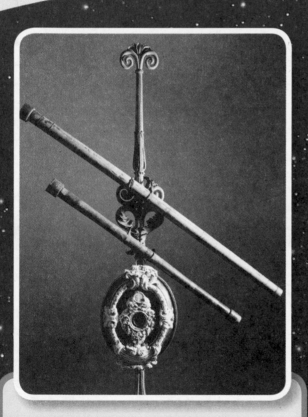

In 1609, the astronomer Galileo invented a new telescope. He used the telescope to study space.

Telescopes today have more parts than the first telescopes had. They are made out of different materials, too.

Telescope Timeline

The telescope has changed since 1609. What do you think the telescope will look like in 50 years? Draw your idea.

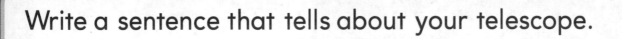

Write a sentence that tells about your telescope.

_____

_____

Build On It!

Build your own telescope. Complete **Improvise It: Telescope** on the Inquiry Flipchart.

Name _____

Essential Question

How Can We Model Day and Night?

TEKS **2.2A** ask questions about organisms, objects, and events during observations and investigations **2.2B** plan and conduct descriptive investigations such as how organisms grow **2.2D** record and organize data using pictures, numbers, and words **2.2E** communicate observations and justify explanations using student-generated data from simple descriptive investigations **2.8D** observe, describe, and record patterns of objects in the sky, including the appearance of the moon

Set a Purpose

Tell what you want to do.

_____

Think About the Procedure

1 What does the globe model?

_____

2 What does the flashlight model?

_____

_____

3 Why do you have to spin the globe?

_____

_____

Record Your Data

Write what you observe.

What does the model show when the place you live is in the light?	
What does the model show when the place you live is in the dark?	

Draw Conclusions

Use your model to explain why Earth has daytime and nighttime.

_____

_____

_____

Ask More Questions

What other questions could you ask about day and night?

_____

_____

_____

Name _____

Vocabulary Review

Use the terms in the box to complete the sentences.

> constellation
> orbit
> rotates

TEKS 2.8D

1. When a planet spins all the way around, it _____.

TEKS 2.8D

2. A group of stars that forms a pattern is called a(n) _____.

TEKS 2.8D

3. The path of a planet around the sun is a(n) _____.

Science Concepts

Fill in the letter of the choice that best answers the question.

TEKS 2.8D

4. How often does the pattern of moon phases repeat?

Ⓐ about every 22 days

Ⓑ about every 25 days

Ⓒ about every 29 days

TEKS 2.8D

5. Why do objects in the sky seem to move in patterns?

Ⓐ because Earth rotates

Ⓑ because Earth orbits the sun

Ⓒ because the sun is the closest star to Earth

TEKS 2.8D

6. Which describes motion in the solar system?

Ⓐ Earth orbits around the other planets.

Ⓑ The planets orbit around the sun.

Ⓒ The sun orbits around the moon.

TEKS 2.8D

7. Look at this umbrella and its shadow.

What time was this picture **most likely** taken?

Ⓐ early morning

Ⓑ early afternoon

Ⓒ early evening

TEKS 2.8D

8. In which phase do we see most of the moon?

Ⓐ first quarter moon

Ⓑ full moon

Ⓒ third quarter moon

TEKS 2.8D

9. How does the pattern of the sun affect the appearance of shadows?

Ⓐ It causes shadows to become shorter or longer.

Ⓑ It causes shadows to become darker or lighter.

Ⓒ It causes shadows to disappear.

TEKS 2.8D

10. What kind of object is at the center of the solar system?

(A) a moon

(B) a planet

(C) a star

TEKS 2.8D

11. This is the moon you saw in the sky last night.

Which moon would you see in about one month?

(A) first quarter moon

(B) full moon

(C) new moon

TEKS 2.8D

12. What object is shown below?

(A) a constellation

(B) a moon

(C) a star

TEKS 2.8D

13. About how long does it take Earth to rotate one time?

(A) 24 hours

(B) 24 days

(C) 24 years

Inquiry and the Big Idea

Write the answers to these questions.

TEKS 2.8D

14. Look at this picture.

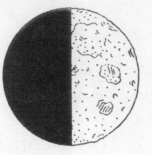

a. Describe the phase of the moon the picture shows.

_____

_____

b. In about how many days will the moon be in the same phase? Explain.

_____

_____

c. Why do people on Earth see the moon in a pattern of phases?

_____

_____

_____

Animal and Plant Needs

Big Idea

Living things have basic needs that must be met.

TEKS 2.2A, 2.2B, 2.2C, 2.2D, 2.2E, 2.9A, 2.10A, 2.10B

sunflowers

I Wonder Why

The sunflowers all face the sun. Why?
Turn the page to find out.

Here's Why

Plants, such as sunflowers, need sunlight to live. They face the sun to get as much sunlight as they can.

In this unit, you will explore this Big Idea, the Essential Questions, and the Investigations on the Inquiry Flipchart.

Levels of Inquiry Key ■ DIRECTED ■ GUIDED ■ INDEPENDENT

Track Your Progress

Big Idea Living things have basic needs that must be met.

Essential Questions

Now I Get the Big Idea!

Science Notebook

Before you begin each lesson, be sure to write your thoughts about the Essential Question.

© Houghton Mifflin Harcourt Publishing Company (tr) ©Bernard Van Berg (inset) ©Karen Su/Corbis; (border) ©Nibsc/Age Fotostock

TEKS **2.9A** identify the basic needs of plants and animals **2.10A** observe, record, and compare how the physical characteristics and behaviors of animals help them meet their basic needs such as fins help fish move and balance in the water

Lesson **1**

Essential Question

What Are Animal Needs?

Engage Your Brain!

Find the answer to the question in the lesson.

How is a frog like a human?

Both need food

to _____ .

Active Reading

Lesson Vocabulary

1 Preview the lesson.

2 Write the 5 vocabulary terms here.

_____   _____

_____
                                 _____

_____

Just the Basics

Animals are living things. Humans are living things, too. Animals and humans have basic needs. **Basic needs** are things that a living thing needs to live and grow. Living things must meet their basic needs in order to **survive**, or stay alive.

What basic need are these animals getting?

Active Reading

Find the sentence that tells the meaning of **basic needs**. Draw a line under the sentence.

Animals need water to survive.

Water Everywhere

Humans need water, too. Drinking water helps us survive. Water is also in other things we drink, such as milk and juice.

The water in this drink helps the girl get what she needs.

▶ Identify something that both animals and humans need.

_____

_____

It's in the Air!

Living things need oxygen to survive. Humans and many animals use body parts called **lungs** to get oxygen from the air. Humans and these animals take in the air through their mouths and noses.

Put a hand on your chest and take a deep breath. Can you feel your lungs taking in air?

This boy is swimming underwater. He is using a snorkel.

▶ How do lungs help some animals meet their needs?

_____

_____

It's in the Water!

Some animals, such as fish, use gills to take in oxygen. **Gills** are parts of an animal that take in oxygen from the water. Can you find the gill on the side of the fish's head?

▶ Label the part of the fish that takes in oxygen.

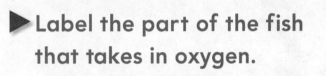

_____

© Houghton Mifflin Harcourt Publishing Company   (b) ©Tom Brakefield/Corbis

Do the Math!
Interpret a Table

Animal Breathing Rates

Use the chart to answer the questions.

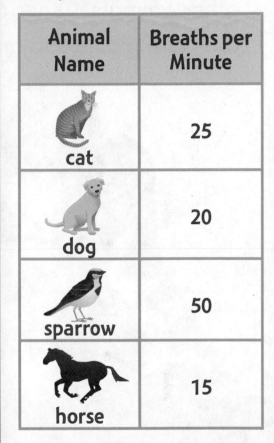

Animal Name	Breaths per Minute
cat	25
dog	20
sparrow	50
horse	15

1. How many more breaths per minute does a sparrow take than a cat?

_____

2. How many more breaths per minute does a dog take than a horse?

_____

Food for Thought

Food is an important need for animals and humans. Food helps animals and humans grow and change. Some animals eat plants. Some eat other animals. Other animals and humans may eat both plants and animals.

A giraffe eats the leaves from trees.

▶ Identify three basic needs of animals.

_____

_____

Protection for All

Animals need space to move, find food, and grow. Humans and many animals also need shelter. A **shelter** is a safe place to live.

Humans also need something that animals do not need. We need clothes to protect our bodies from cold and rainy weather.

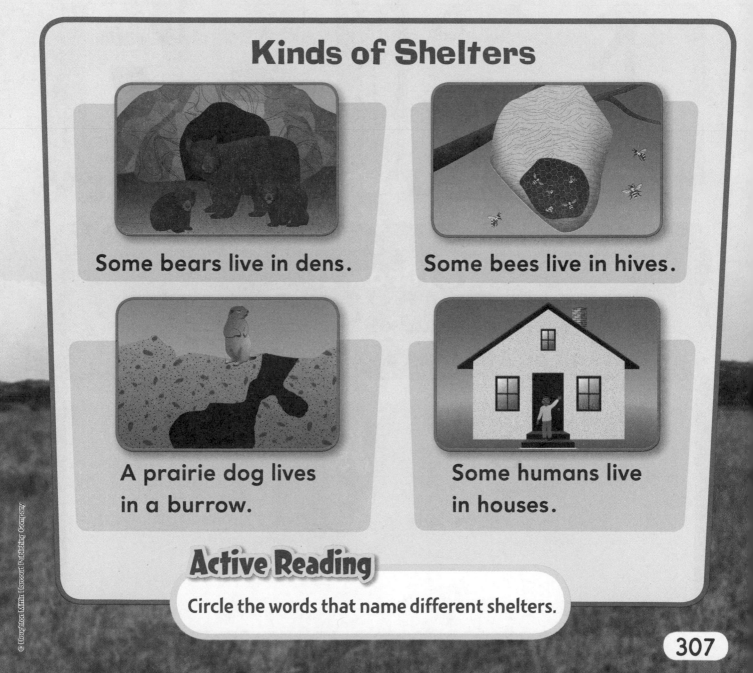

Kinds of Shelters

Some bears live in dens.

Some bees live in hives.

A prairie dog lives in a burrow.

Some humans live in houses.

Active Reading

Circle the words that name different shelters.

Sum It Up!

1 Circle It!

Circle the living thing that does **not** use lungs to get oxygen.

2 Mark It!

Cross out the thing that humans do **not** need to survive.

3 Draw It!

Identify a basic need of animals. Draw an animal meeting that need.

Name _____

Word Play

Read the words and the clues.
Write the word that goes with each clue.

| lungs | gills | shelter | survive | oxygen |

1 I am a safe place to live. ___ ___ ___ ___ ___ ___ ___

2 We are the body parts that you use to take in oxygen.

___ ___ ___ ___ ___

3 I mean to stay alive. ___ ___ ___ ___ ___ ___ ___

4 We are the body parts that fish and tadpoles use to stay alive in water.

___ ___ ___ ___ ___

5 I am in the air you breathe. ___ ___ ___ ___ ___ ___

Apply Concepts

Complete the Venn diagram. Show how animal needs and plant needs are alike and different.

Animal Needs   Both   Plant Needs

Complete the sentence.
Tell about the main idea of this lesson.
Basic needs are the things that animals and plants

need to _____.

Family Members: Talk about animals that you and your child have or know. Ask your child to tell how those animals meet their basic needs.

TEKS **2.3A** identify and explain a problem in his/her own words and propose a task and solution for the problem such as lack of water in a habitat

S.T.E.M.

Engineering and Technology

Tool Time

How We Use Tools

Tools are objects that people use to make a job easier. People can use tools to meet needs.

One need is shelter. A shelter may be a house. People use many tools to build a house.

drill

hammer

311

The Best Tool for the Job

Draw a line to match each tool to show how it is used.

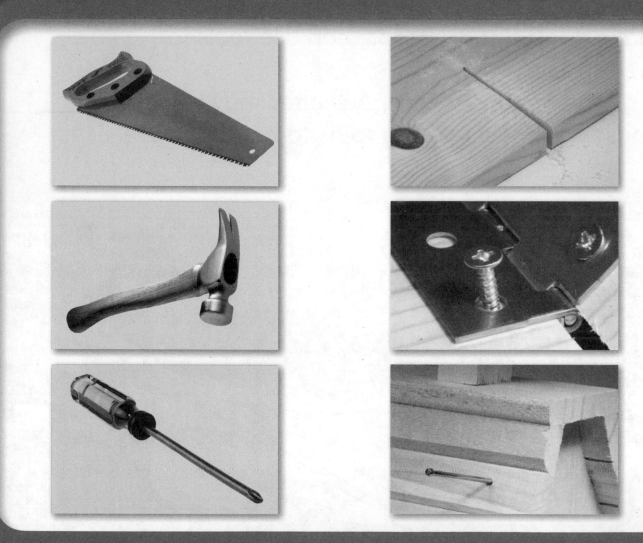

Build On It!

You can design your own tool. Complete **Design It: A New Tool** on the Inquiry Flipchart.

TEKS 2.9A identify the basic needs of plants and animals 2.10B observe, record, and compare how the physical characteristics of plants help them meet their basic needs such as stems carry water throughout the plant

Essential Question

What Are Plant Needs?

Engage Your Brain!

Find the answer to the question in the lesson.

What do you know about a pumpkin this big?

Its

_____

were met.

Active Reading

Lesson Vocabulary

1 Preview the lesson.

2 Write the vocabulary term here.

_____

Inquiry Flipchart p. 43 — Block the Light/Airtight Seal

Plant Needs

Plants are living things. Like all living things, plants have basic needs. What happens if a plant does not meet its basic needs? It may stop growing. It may turn brown or begin to droop. It may die.

Active Reading

The main idea is the most important idea about something. Draw two lines under the main idea.

These plants are meeting their basic needs.

▶ Identify the basic need the boy is giving the plants.

_____

People can help plants meet their basic needs.

Wonderful Water

Plants need water. Do you know how they get it? A plant's roots take in water from the soil. Water is a basic need that helps plants live and grow.

Light and Airy

Do you wonder why people put some potted plants by windows? Plants need sunlight to grow. They also need air and water. Plants use air, water, and sunlight to make their own food.

Active Reading

Underline the sentence that tells what plants need to make food.

How are these plants getting what they need?

Nutrients and Space

Plants need nutrients from the soil. **Nutrients** are substances that help plants grow. Growing plants need more nutrients and water. Their roots grow and spread to get more of these things. Plants need enough space for their roots, stems, and leaves to grow.

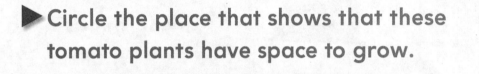

▶ Circle the place that shows that these tomato plants have space to grow.

Sum It Up!

1 Mark It!

Cross out the thing that a plant does not need to grow.

2 Solve It!

Fill in the blank.

I am all around you but you can't see me. I am something all living things need.

What am I?

_____

3 Draw It!

Draw a picture of a plant. Label the picture to show that the plant is getting what it needs.

Name _____

Word Play

Find and circle the words in this word search. Then answer the question.

| sunlight | water | soil | air | space | nutrients |

```
s  u  n  l  i  g  h  t  a  s
p  a  e  k  w  a  t  r  b  o
a  i  r  y  a  n  s  o  i  l
c  p  c  e  t  l  d  o  u  i
e  t  s  p  e  c  a  t  m  n
a  n  u  t  r  i  e  n  t  s
```

What are the things that plants must meet to live and grow?

_____

Identify what plants need. Complete the word web.

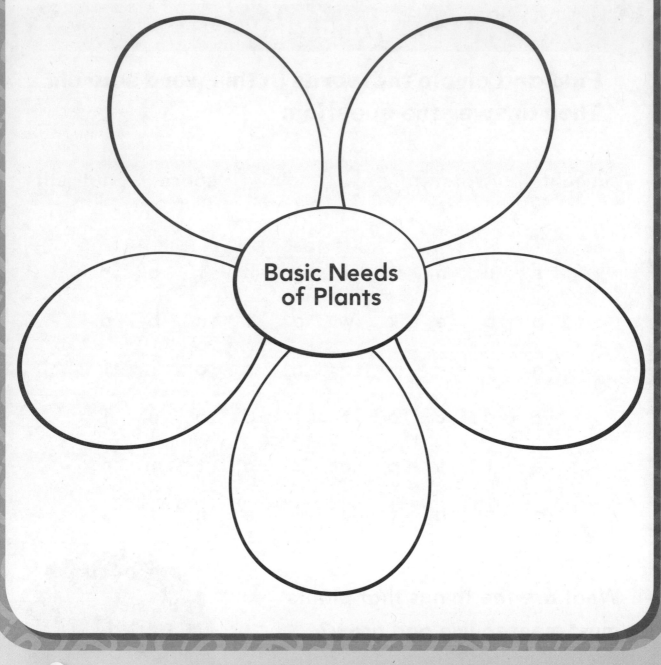

Basic Needs of Plants

Take It Home!

Family Members: With your child, talk about the plants that grow in or around your home. Ask your child to tell how the plants get the things they need to grow.

TEKS **2.2A** ask questions about organisms, objects, and events during observations and investigations **2.2B** plan and conduct descriptive investigations such as how organisms grow **2.2C** collect data from observations using simple equipment such as hand lenses, primary balances, thermometers, and non-standard measurement tools **2.2D** record and organize data using pictures, numbers, and words **2.2E** communicate observations and justify explanations using student-generated data from simple descriptive investigations **2.9A** identify the basic needs of plants and animals

Name _____

Essential Question

What Do Plants Need to Grow?

Set a Purpose

Tell what you want to find out.

_____

_____

Think About the Procedure

❶ What will you observe?

_____

_____

❷ How will you treat the plants differently?

_____

_____

Record Your Data

Use your data to communicate your observations.

My Observations			
Number of Days	Plant A	Plant B	Plant C
Day 2			
Day 5			
Day 7			
Day 10			

Draw Conclusions

❶ Do plants need water to grow? Use your data to tell how you know.

_____

❷ Can a plant get too much water? Use your data to tell how you know.

_____

Ask More Questions

What are some other questions about what plants need to grow?

_____

_____

Ask a Bugologist

What is a bugologist?
A bugologist is a scientist who studies insects. We look at how insects act. We study their life cycles. We try to find out how insects affect people and the environment.

How do you work?
Some bugologists work outdoors. We collect and observe insects. Other bugologists work in labs or classrooms.

What tools do you use?
We collect insects with nets and traps. Jars and bags hold what we find. We use a hand lens or a microscope to see insects up close.

Now It's Your Turn!

▶ Explore what scientists do. What question would you ask a bugologist?

_____

_____

_____

Be a Bugologist

Insects have three body parts and six legs. They also have a hard outer body covering. Look at the picture. It shows the parts of an insect. Can you find the insects below?

antenna

leg

body parts

▶ Circle the insects. Use the picture to help you.

Unit 8 Review

Vocabulary Review

Use the terms in the box to complete the sentences.

nutrients
shelter
survive

TEKS 2.9A

1. A _____ is a safe place where an animal lives.

TEKS 2.9A

2. Living things must meet their basic needs in order to _____.

TEKS 2.9A

3. Substances that help plants grow are _____.

Science Concepts

Fill in the letter of the choice that best answers the question.

TEKS 2.9A

4. What body part do fish need to take in oxygen from water?

   Ⓐ gills

   Ⓑ lungs

   Ⓒ roots

TEKS 2.9A

5. What do plants need in order to make their own food?

   Ⓐ air, water, and sunlight

   Ⓑ shelter, sunlight, and water

   Ⓒ nutrients, shelter, and sunlight

TEKS 2.9A

6. Tina does an experiment with two plants of the same kind. She gives Plant 1 fresh water. She gives Plant 2 salt water. The pictures show the results of Tina's experiment.

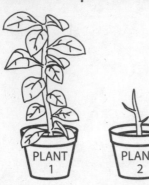

What can you infer?

Ⓐ These plants grow better with salt water than with fresh water.

Ⓑ These plants grow better with fresh water than with salt water.

Ⓒ These plants grow the same with either fresh water or salt water.

TEKS 2.9A

7. How does a plant get nutrients?

Ⓐ from air

Ⓑ from seeds

Ⓒ from soil

TEKS 2.2A, 2.9A

8. Kara observes one of her plants turning brown and drooping. What question should Kara ask about the plant?

Ⓐ What basic needs of this plant are not being met?

Ⓑ What kind of plant am I growing?

Ⓒ How are plants different from animals?

TEKS 2.9A

9. What basic need is the animal meeting?

Ⓐ the need for air

Ⓑ the need for food

Ⓒ the need for shelter

TEKS 2.9A

10. Look at the picture.

Tasha has two plants. She waters Plant A every day. She does not water Plant C. What will happen to Plant C?

(A) Plant C will die.

(B) Plant C will grow faster than Plant A.

(C) Plant C will grow larger than Plant A.

TEKS 2.9A

11. How are the needs of plants and animals alike?

(A) Animals and plants both need sunlight to make their own food.

(B) Animals and plants both need air and water to survive.

(C) Animals and plants both need lungs to breathe.

TEKS 2.9A

12. Which is something that only humans need?

(A) clothes

(B) food

(C) oxygen

Inquiry and the Big Idea

Write the answers to these questions.

TEKS 2.9A

13. a. Identify two basic needs of plants and animals.

_____

b. Identify something that all living things need to survive.
   Compare how plants and animals meet that need.

_____

_____

c. Name something animals need that plants do not need.

_____

TEKS 2.2B, 2.9A

14. Tell how you would plan an investigation to show that plants
   need water to survive.

_____

_____

_____

Environments for Living Things

impala and
red-billed
oxpecker

Big Idea

Living things must
meet their needs in
their environments.

TEKS 2.2A, 2.2B, 2.2C, 2.2D, 2.2E, 2.2F,
2.9B, 2.9C, 2.10A, 2.10B

I Wonder Why

The bird is picking bugs off the
impala. Why?
Turn the page to find out.

Here's Why The bird eats the bugs for food.

In this unit, you will explore this Big Idea, the Essential Questions, and the Investigations on the Inquiry Flipchart.

Science Notebook

Before you begin each lesson, be sure to write your thoughts about the Essential Question.

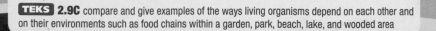

TEKS 2.9C compare and give examples of the ways living organisms depend on each other and on their environments such as food chains within a garden, park, beach, lake, and wooded area

Lesson **1**

Essential Question

How Do Plants and Animals Need One Another?

Engage Your Brain!

Find the answer to the question in the lesson.

This bat drinks from the plant. How is the bat also helping the plant?

The bat spreads

_____ .

Active Reading

Lesson Vocabulary

1 Preview the lesson.

2 Write the 3 vocabulary terms here.

_____   _____

_____

In Your Place

Plants and animals use living and nonliving things to meet their needs. They get the things they need from their environment. All the living and nonliving things in a place make up an **environment**. Plants and animals need an environment where there is water, food, air, and space.

Active Reading

Find the sentence that tells the meaning of **environment**. Draw a line under the sentence.

Plants and animals need an environment where they can find water.

Plants and animals need air in their environment.

Plants need an environment where they can get sunlight to make food. Animals need an environment where they can find food.

Plants and animals need an environment where they have space to live and grow. Some animals need to find shelter in their environment.

▶ Give an example of how living things depend on their environment. Then compare how plants and animals get food in their environment.

_____

_____

_____

Getting Help

Animals depend on plants in their environment to meet their needs. Many animals use plants for shelter. Some animals hide in plants. Other animals live in plants or use them to build homes.

Active Reading

A detail is a fact about a main idea. Draw one line under a detail. Draw an arrow to the main idea it tells about.

The bird uses plants to build a nest.

A lion hides in tall grass.

Animals need to breathe air to get oxygen, a gas in the air. Plants give off oxygen. Some animals use plants for food. Some animals eat other animals that eat plants.

Ants find both food and shelter in the thorns of this tree.

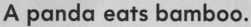

A panda eats bamboo.

► Compare ways animals depend on plants.

_____

_____

_____

_____

_____

Giving Help

Plants depend on animals in their environment. Animals may help plants reproduce, or make new plants. Some animals carry fruits to new places. There, the seeds inside the fruits may grow into new plants.

Active Reading

The main idea is the most important idea about something. Draw two lines under the main idea.

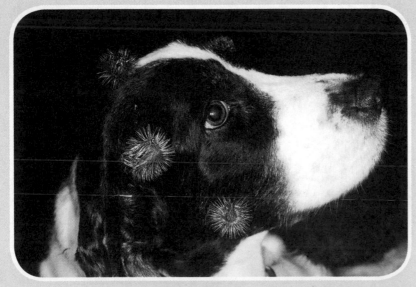

The dog spreads seeds that are inside the burrs on its fur.

Some animals spread pollen for plants. **Pollen** is a powder that flowers need to make seeds. Pollen may stick to an animal. The animal carries the pollen from flower to flower. This helps plants make new plants.

As a bat drinks the flower nectar, pollen rubs off on the bat.

A woodpecker moves acorns with its beak. Seeds are inside the acorns.

▶ Give examples of how animals help plants reproduce.

_____

_____

_____

A beetle carries pollen on its body.

Eat Up!

These pictures show a food chain. A **food chain** shows how energy moves from plants to animals. Follow the arrows. Look at how living things depend on one another in a lake food chain.

Food chains start with sunlight and plants. In this food chain, the water plants use sunlight to make food.

An eagle eats the turtle.

A turtle eats the water plants.

▶ Draw what is missing from the first step of this wooded area food chain.

At the Beach

There are food chains in many different environments. Look at how living things depend on each other in a beach food chain.

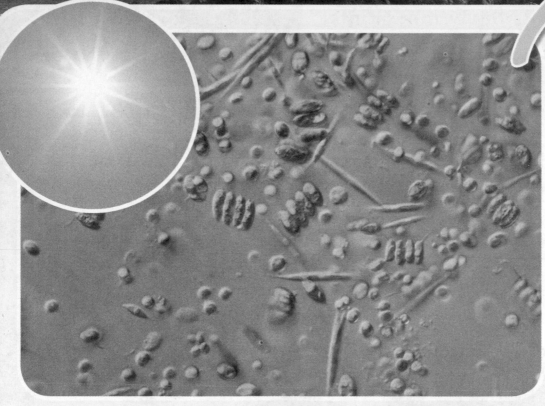

A beach food chain starts with sunlight and plants or plant-like living things. The plants or plant-like living things use sunlight to make food.

A rockfish eats the krill.

Krill, a kind of ocean animal, eat plant-like living things.

Do the Math!
Solve a Problem

Read the word problem. Then solve it. Show your work.

A copper rockfish can grow as long as 55 centimeters. A tiger rockfish can grow as long as 30 centimeters. How much longer can a copper rockfish grow than a tiger rockfish?

____ centimeters

Sum It Up!

① Label It!

Write <u>water</u>, <u>food</u>, or <u>shelter</u> to tell what each living thing is getting from its environment.

_____   _____   _____   _____

② Order It!

Number the steps in this food chain to show the correct order.

_____   _____   _____

Name _____

Word Play

Read each clue below. Then unscramble the letters to write the correct answer.

| environment | oxygen | pollen | food chain |

1. a gas in the air that animals need to survive

   nxyego _____

2. all the living and nonliving things in a place

   nervnitnmeo _____

3. shows how energy moves from plants to animals

   ofod   inhca _____

4. flowers need this to make seeds

   lonpel _____

Apply Concepts

Use words from the word bank to complete the chart.

shelter   oxygen   seeds   food   pollen

Ways Animals Use Plants	Ways Animals Help Plants
When animals build nests, they use plants for _____.	Animals help carry _____ to new places.
Animals eat plants as _____.	Animals spread _____ that sticks to their bodies.
Animals need _____ that plants give off.	

Take It Home!

Family Members: Take a walk outside with your child. Help your child observe animals using plants.

TEKS **2.9B** identify factors in the environment, including temperature and precipitation, that affect growth and behavior . . . of living things **2.10A** observe, record, and compare how the physical characteristics and behaviors of animals help them meet their basic needs . . . **2.10B** observe, record, and compare how the physical characteristics of plants help them meet their basic needs . . .

Essential Question

How Are Living Things Adapted to Their Environments?

🧠 Engage Your Brain!

Find the answer to the question in the lesson.

Find the caterpillar. How do its color and shape help it stay safe?

They help it

_____

Active Reading

Lesson Vocabulary

1 Preview the lesson.

2 Write the vocabulary term here.

_____

Survival Skills

Plants live almost everywhere. Some places they live are dry. Other places are wet and shady. Plants have ways to meet their basic needs where they live. These ways are called adaptations. An **adaptation** is something that helps a living thing survive in its environment.

Water lilies have long stems that let their leaves reach the water's surface. There, the leaves get sunlight.

▶ Observe this plant and its parts. Circle the kind of environment where it would best survive.

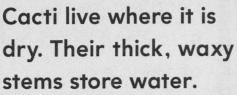

dry   wet

Cacti live where it is dry. Their thick, waxy stems store water.

Rain forest plants have very large leaves. These leaves help the plants get sunlight in the shady forest.

Animals At Home

Animals also have adaptations to help them survive in their environments. They may live where there is little food. They may live where it is very cold. Their adaptations help them meet their basic needs where they live.

Active Reading

The main idea is the most important idea about something. Draw two lines under the main idea.

Camels live where it is dry and sandy. Long eyelashes help keep sand out of their eyes.

Penguins live on ice and in cold water. A thick layer of fat keeps them warm.

Giraffes have long tongues to pull leaves off trees.

▶ Observe this animal and its parts. Circle the kind of environment where it would best survive.

dry, sandy

cold water

Plant Protection

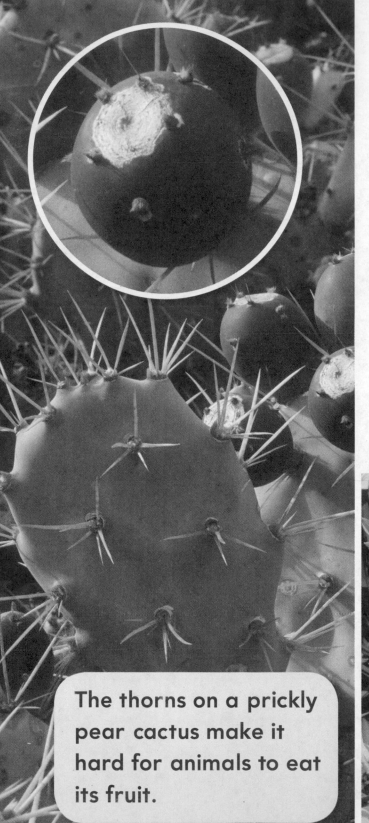

The thorns on a prickly pear cactus make it hard for animals to eat its fruit.

Living things also have adaptations to protect themselves. Plant adaptations help keep plants safe from animals that might eat them. Some of these adaptations are thorns, bad taste, and quick movement.

Daffodils taste bad. Animals do not like to eat them.

The leaves of the mimosa plant fold quickly when touched. This may knock off insects that want to eat the leaves.

▶ Name two plant adaptations that protect plants from animals.

_____

_____

_____

_____

Animal Protection

Many animals must protect themselves from other animals. They have adaptations to help them stay safe. These adaptations help protect animals from other animals that want to eat them.

Active Reading

A detail is a fact about a main idea. Draw one line under a detail. Draw an arrow to the main idea it tells about.

Skunks can spray a bad smell. The bad smell scares off other animals.

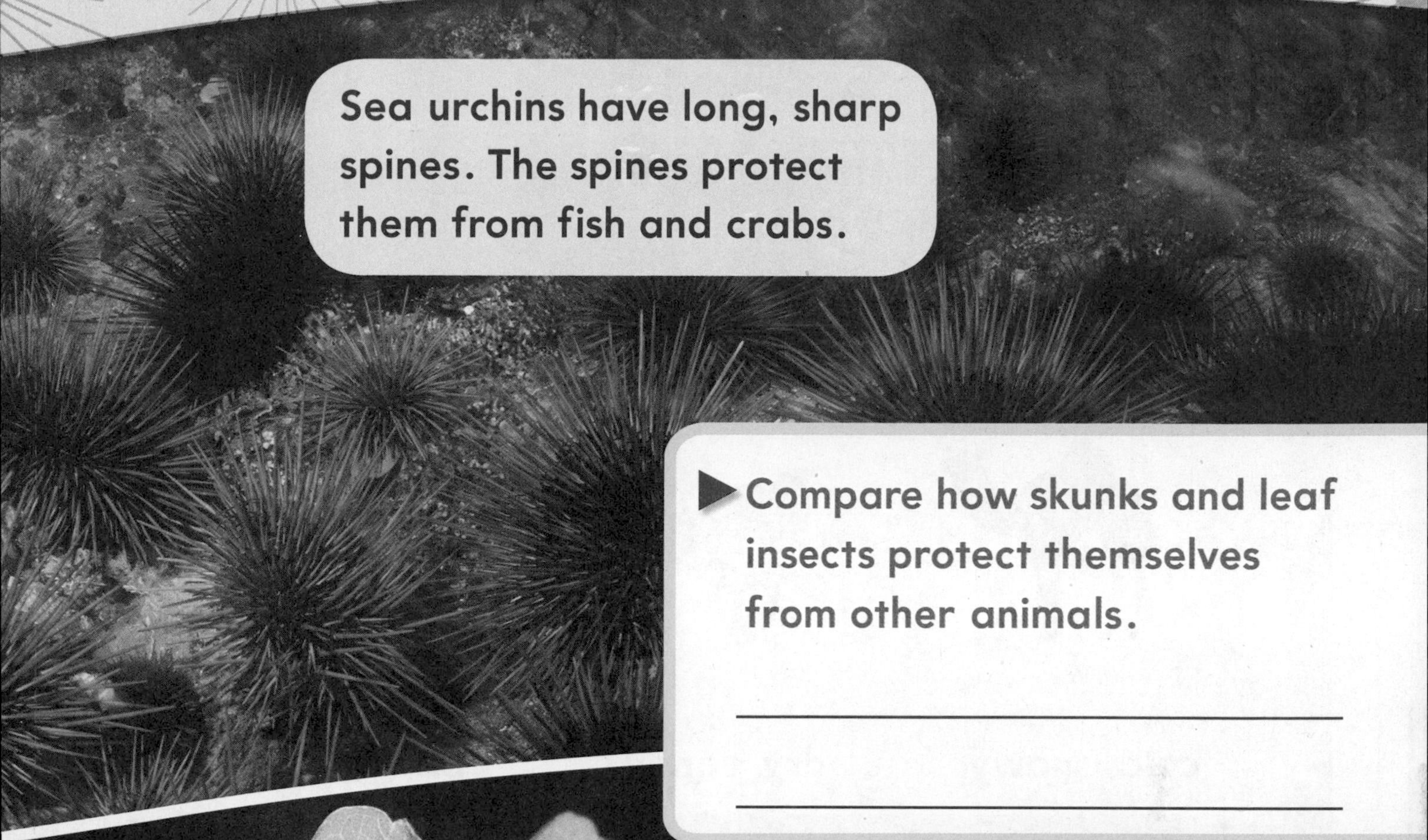

Sea urchins have long, sharp spines. The spines protect them from fish and crabs.

Compare how skunks and leaf insects protect themselves from other animals.

_____

_____

The leaf insect looks like the leaf. This helps the insect hide.

Sum It Up!

① Match It!

Match each living thing to the environment where it lives.

cold, snowy   dry, sandy   wet, shady

② Write It!

Compare how each living thing protects itself.

_____   _____   _____

Name _____

Word Play

Define the word adaptation. Then list adaptations that help plants and animals survive.

adaptation:

_____

_____

Plants	Animals
large leaves	fat

Apply Concepts

Write two details that go with the main idea. Include details about two different adaptations.

Main Idea

Adaptations help living things survive in different environments.

Detail	Detail

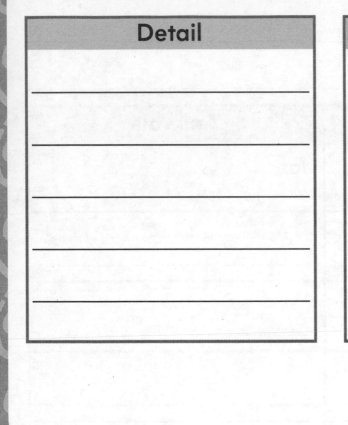

Family Members: Ask your child to describe some animal adaptations. Discuss how those adaptations help the animals survive.

Take It Home!

Name _____

TEKS **2.2A** ask questions about organisms . . .during observations and investigations **2.2B** plan and conduct descriptive investigations such as how organisms grow **2.2C** collect data from observations using simple equipment . . . **2.2D** record and organize data using pictures, numbers, and words **2.2E** communicate observations and justify explanations using student-generated data from simple descriptive investigations **2.2F** compare results of investigations with what students and scientists know about the world **2.10B** observe, record, and compare how the physical characteristics of plants help them meet their needs such as stems carry water throughout the plant

Essential Question

Can Plants Survive in Different Environments?

Set a Purpose

Write what you want to find out.

_____

Make a Prediction

Write a prediction about what you think will happen.

_____

_____

Think About the Procedure

❶ Why will you water the **desert** plant only once?

_____

❷ Why will you water the **rain forest** plant three times a day?

_____

Record Your Data

Use your data to communicate your observations.

Date	Desert Plant	Rain Forest Plant

Draw Conclusions

Compare your results with what you predicted. Can a plant from one environment live in a different environment? Use your data to tell how you know.

_____

_____

Ask More Questions

What other questions could you ask about plants in different environments?

_____

_____

Go with the Flow

Moving Water

People need water to drink and grow crops. But some places do not have enough water for people to use. People use technology to move water to where they live. Then they get the water they need. People have moved water for many, many years.

Today, people use pipes to move water. Pipes bring water to homes and workplaces.

In the past, people used stone bridges to move water. The water moved from lakes and springs into cities.

Water Ways

Look at ways people have moved water over the years.

What problem do people solve by moving water?
Why do you think they have changed the way they
move water?

_____

_____

_____

Build On It!

Design a way to bring water to a place. Complete
Design It: For the Birds on the Inquiry Flipchart.

Ask an Environmental Scientist

Now It's Your Turn!

▶ What question would you ask an environmental scientist?

_____

_____

_____

What do environmental scientists do?
We study the harmful effects to different kinds of environments.

How do environmental scientists help wildlife?
We find problems that affect wildlife and people in the environments. We figure out ways to solve those problems.

Sometimes people can harm an environment. For example, a factory may put waste into a stream. This may kill fish. We help the factory find other ways to get rid of its waste.

Making Environments Better

► Draw or write the answer to each question.

1 What do you think is most interesting about what environmental scientists do?

2 What might be difficult about what they do?

3 Why are environmental scientists important?

4 Think about being an environmental scientist. Draw an environment you would like to study.

1

2

3

4

Vocabulary Review

Use the terms in the box to complete the sentences.

adaptation
environment
food chain

TEKS 2.9C

1. A _____ shows how energy moves from one living thing to another.

TEKS 2.9C

2. All of the living and nonliving things in a place make up an

_____.

TEKS 2.10A

3. Humps help camels survive in their environment. Humps are an

_____.

Science Concepts

Fill in the letter of the choice that best answers the question.

TEKS 2.10B

4. What adaptation helps a cactus meet its needs in its environment?

   Ⓐ long stems

   Ⓑ thick stems

   Ⓒ large leaves

TEKS 2.9C

5. Which begins every food chain?

   Ⓐ animals and plants

   Ⓑ animals and food

   Ⓒ sunlight and plants

TEKS 2.9C

6. This picture shows the steps in a food chain.

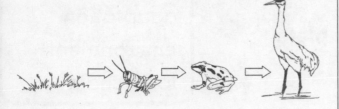

Which statement about this food chain is **true**?

Ⓐ Frogs eat grasshoppers.

Ⓑ Grasshoppers eat frogs.

Ⓒ Frogs and grasshoppers eat each other.

TEKS 2.10B

7. A plant has adaptations for living in a wet, shady environment. What will **most likely** happen if it is moved to a sunny, dry place?

Ⓐ The plant will die.

Ⓑ The plant will grow better.

Ⓒ The plant will grow as well.

TEKS 2.9C

8. How do animals help plants meet their needs?

Ⓐ by making food for them

Ⓑ by spreading their seeds and pollen

Ⓒ by giving them shelter and oxygen

TEKS 2.10A

9. Look at the adaptations of this polar bear.

Where would the bear best survive?

Ⓐ hot, dry environment

Ⓑ cold, icy environment

Ⓒ warm, wet environment

TEKS 2.2B

10. You do a test that shows rain forest plants need water to live. How can you check that your results were correct?

Ⓐ You can do the test again using desert plants.

Ⓑ You can do the test again the same way.

Ⓒ You can do the test in a different environment.

TEKS 2.9C

11. Beetles spread pollen as they move from plant to plant. What does this show?

Ⓐ Plants depend on animals to reproduce.

Ⓑ Plants depend on animals for food.

Ⓒ Plants depend on animals for shelter.

TEKS 2.9C

12. How is the animal using the tree in this picture?

Ⓐ It is using the tree for food.

Ⓑ It is using the tree for water.

Ⓒ It is using the tree for shelter.

Inquiry and the Big Idea
Write the answers to these questions.

TEKS 2.10A

13. Describe two adaptations that would help an animal survive in a cold environment. Explain your answer.

_____

_____

TEKS 2.9C

14. Look at this picture.

a. What does this picture show? What do the arrows show?

_____

_____

b. How does the frog depend on other living things to survive? Use the picture to explain.

_____

_____

_____

Animal and Plant Characteristics

Big Idea

Living things look like their parents. Living things have parts that help them meet their basic needs.

TEKS 2.2A, 2.2B, 2.2D, 2.2E, 2.4B, 2.10A, 2.10B, 2.10C

sea turtle

I Wonder Why

Mother sea turtles bury their eggs in the sand. Why?
Turn the page to find out.

Here's Why Mother turtles need to keep their eggs warm and protected for the young turtles to hatch.

In this unit, you will explore this Big Idea, the Essential Questions, and the Investigations on the Inquiry Flipchart.

Levels of Inquiry Key ■ DIRECTED ■ GUIDED ■ INDEPENDENT

Track Your Progress

Big Idea Living things look like their parents. Living things have parts that help them meet their basic needs.

Essential Questions

Now I Get the Big Idea!

Science Notebook
Before you begin each lesson, be sure to write your thoughts about the Essential Question.

TEKS 2.10A observe, record, and compare how the physical characteristics and behaviors of animals help them meet their basic needs such as fins help fish move and balance in the water

Lesson 1

Essential Question

What Are Some Kinds of Animals?

Engage Your Brain!

Find the answer to the question in the lesson.

A penguin cannot fly. But it's still a bird. Why?

It _____ .

Active Reading

Lesson Vocabulary

❶ Preview the lesson.

❷ Write the 6 vocabulary terms here.

_____ _____

_____ _____

_____ _____

Animal Stars

Many kinds of animals live on Earth. Animals are many different shapes, colors, and sizes. Different animals have different body parts and coverings. Animals have their young in different ways, too. Here are some stars of the animal world!

Active Reading

The main idea is the most important idea about something. Draw two lines under the main idea.

Some animals lay eggs.

Other animals give birth to live young.

Animal Body Parts

Fins help fish swim and balance. They also help fish steer.

Suction cups help the frog climb and hold on.

An elephant can use its trunk to grab and lift. It can also use its trunk to drink water.

▶ Compare how fish and frogs use their parts to move.

_____

_____

_____

_____

By a Hair

A **mammal** has hair or fur that covers its skin. Most mammal mothers give birth to live young. The young drink milk from their mothers' bodies. Mammals breathe air. They take in oxygen through lungs.

Active Reading

Find the sentence that tells the meaning of **mammal**. Draw a line under the sentence.

Manatees rise to the top of water to breathe air.

Many mammals have legs to move. This antelope uses its legs to run fast.

A Fine Feather

A **bird** has feathers that cover its skin. Birds have wings, too. Feathers and wings help most birds fly. Birds use beaks to get food and build nests. Bird mothers lay eggs to have young.

Not all birds can fly. A kiwi has feathers and wings, but it cannot fly.

This pelican has wide wings. It uses its long, deep beak to scoop fish.

▶ **How do beaks helps birds meet their basic needs?**

_____

_____

Scale Up

A **reptile** has dry skin covered with scales. Most reptiles walk on four legs. Most reptile mothers lay eggs. Most reptile mothers lay their eggs on land.

Snakes are reptiles, but they do not have legs. Some snake mothers give birth to live young.

A tortoise has a hard shell. It can hide in its shell if it senses danger.

On Land and Water

An **amphibian** lives in water and on land. Most amphibians have smooth, wet skin. They lay their eggs in water. Young amphibians live in the water. Most adult amphibians live on land.

This toad is an amphibian, but it has rough, bumpy skin. Its strong back legs help it jump.

This newt is an amphibian. It has smooth, wet skin.

▶ Write where each group lays its eggs.

reptiles	amphibians

A Fish Story

Fish live in water and take in oxygen through gills. Fins help fish swim and balance. Most fish have scales. Most fish lay eggs.

moorish idols

betta

Moorish idols and bettas are fish. They lay eggs in water.

Sharks are fish. They give birth to live young.

As Snug as a Bug

An **insect** has three body parts and six legs. It also has a hard outer body covering, but no bones. Most insects live on land. Many insects can fly.

One part of an insect is its head. Where is the head on these insects?

ladybug

butterfly

grasshopper

▶ Write where each group lives.

fish	insects

Sum It Up!

① Mark It!

Mark an X on each amphibian. Circle each reptile.

② Label It!

Draw a fish. Label how its parts help it move.

③ Match It!

Match the parts to what they do.

fins	help most birds fly
gills	help fish take in oxygen
wings	help fish swim

Name _____

Word Play

Use the words below to label each animal.

fish   amphibian   insect   bird   reptile   mammal

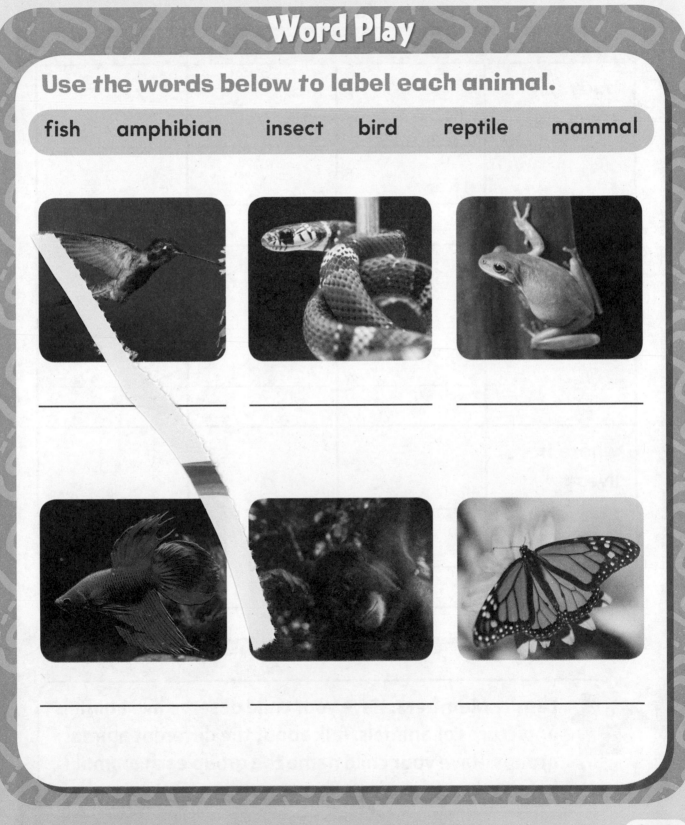

_____   _____   _____

_____   _____   _____

Apply Concepts

Fill in the chart. Show what you know about each animal.

Animals

	manatee	toad	kiwi
body covering	_____ _____	_____ _____	_____ _____
how it has its young	_____ _____	_____ _____	_____ _____
where it lives	_____ _____	_____ _____	_____ _____

Family Members: Have your child observe live animals or pictures of animals. Talk about the different animal groups. Have your child name the group each animal belongs to and explain why.

Take It Home!

TEKS 2.2A ask questions about organisms . . . **2.2B** plan and conduct descriptive investigations . . . **2.2D** record and organize data . . . **2.2E** communicate observations and justify explanations . . . **2.10A** observe, record, and compare how the physical characteristics and behaviors of animals . . .

Name _____

Essential Question

How Do Body Coverings Help Animals?

Set a Purpose

Write what you want to find out during this investigation.

_____

_____

Think About the Procedure

1 What body covering is the shortening like?

_____

_____

2 What body covering is the mitten like?

_____

_____

Record Your Data

Write **warmer** or **colder** to communicate your observations.

❶ The hand in the shortening felt _____ than the other hand.

❷ The hand in the mitten felt _____ than the other hand.

Draw Conclusions

❶ Does fat keep animals warm in cold environments? Use your data to tell how you know.

_____

_____

_____

❷ Does fur keep animals warm? Use your data to tell how you know.

_____

_____

Ask More Questions

What other questions can you ask about animal body coverings?

_____

_____

© Houghton Mifflin Harcourt Publishing Company

Essential Question

How Can We Compare Animal Life Cycles?

Engage Your Brain!

Find the answer to the question in the lesson.

What will this larva grow up to be?

It will become a

_____.

Active Reading

Lesson Vocabulary

1 Preview the lesson.

2 Write the 6 vocabulary terms here.

_____ _____

_____ _____

_____ _____

A Good Start

adult dog

All living things reproduce. When living things **reproduce**, they make more living things of the same kind.

Some young animals, like dogs, look like their parents. Other young animals do not look like their parents. The young frog does not look like the adult frog. It will grow up to look like the adult frog.

young dog

Active Reading

Find the sentence that tells the meaning of **reproduce**. Draw a line under the sentence.

young frog

adult frog

Animals have young in different ways. Some young are born live. Dogs are born live. Other animals hatch from eggs. Frogs hatch from eggs. Look at the chart. How do these animals have young?

Born Live	Hatch from Eggs
dolphin	bird
deer	turtle

▶ Name another animal that is born live.

Lion Roar

Hear Me Roar!

A lion is a mammal. Most mammals give birth to live young. Most young mammals look like their parents.

Every animal changes as it grows. The changes an animal goes through during its life make up its **life cycle**. Let's look at a lion's life cycle.

1

newborn cub

A lion cub is born live. It drinks milk from its mother's body.

2

growing cub

The lion cub gets bigger. It stops drinking milk from its mother.

▶ Read the captions. Circle the words that describe stages of a lion's life cycle.

3

young lion

The young lion learns to hunt.

4

adult lion

An adult lion can live on its own.
It can reproduce.

Ladybug Life

Have you ever seen a ladybug? A ladybug is an insect. It begins life inside an egg. It changes form as it grows to become an adult. This is called metamorphosis. **Metamorphosis** is a series of changes that some animals go through.

2

1

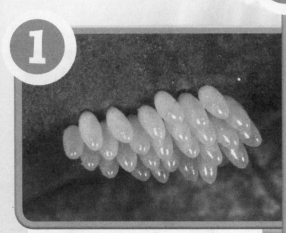

egg

An adult female ladybug lays eggs.

larva

A larva hatches from each egg. A larva is a young insect that looks different from its parents. The larva eats a lot and grows quickly.

► Read the captions to contrast the mammal and ladybug life cycles. Which stages do only ladybugs have? Underline the names of the stages.

③

④

pupa

The larva stops eating. Its skin dries and hardens. The larva becomes a pupa. The pupa goes through changes inside the skin.

adult

An adult ladybug comes out of the skin. It can now reproduce.

Let It Fly

A dragonfly is also an insect. Like a ladybug, it goes through metamorphosis.

Active Reading

Clue words can help you find ways things are alike. *Like* is a clue word. Draw a box around *like*.

1

2

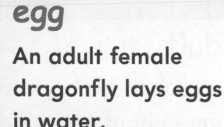

egg

An adult female dragonfly lays eggs in water.

nymph

A nymph hatches from each egg. A nymph is a young dragonfly. It looks a lot like its parents. Dragonfly nymphs live and grow in water.

3

adult

An adult dragonfly can live on land.
It has strong wings! It can reproduce.

▶ Read the captions to contrast the
ladybug and dragonfly life cycles.
What stage do dragonflies have
that ladybugs do not? Underline the
name of the stage.

Sum It Up!

① Circle It!

Which animal hatches from an egg?

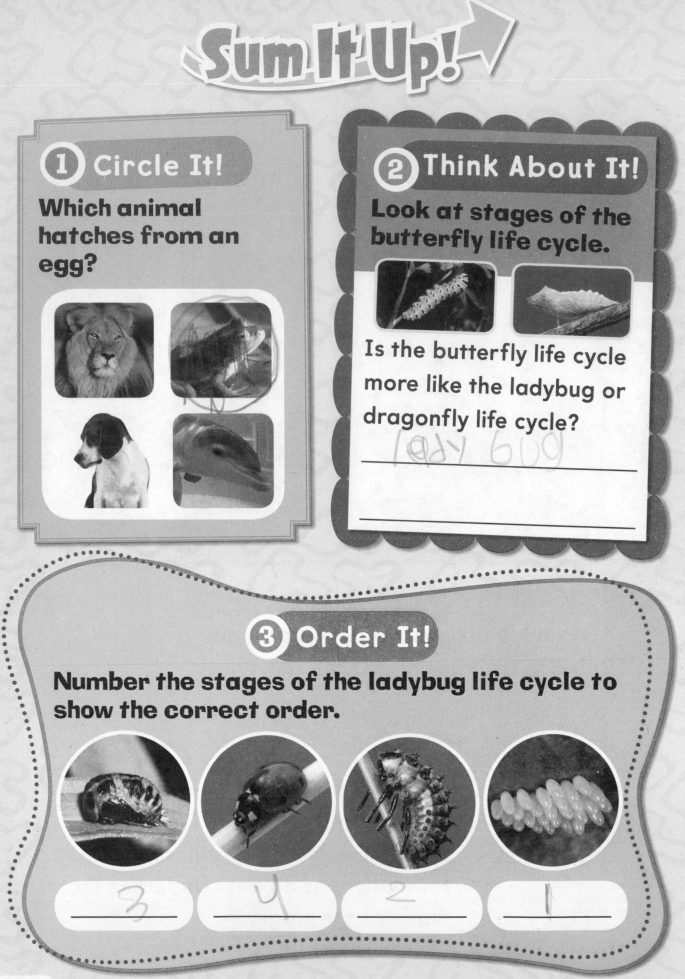

② Think About It!

Look at stages of the butterfly life cycle.

Is the butterfly life cycle more like the ladybug or dragonfly life cycle?

lady bug

③ Order It!

Number the stages of the ladybug life cycle to show the correct order.

3   4   2   1

Name _____

Word Play

Draw lines to match each word with its definition.

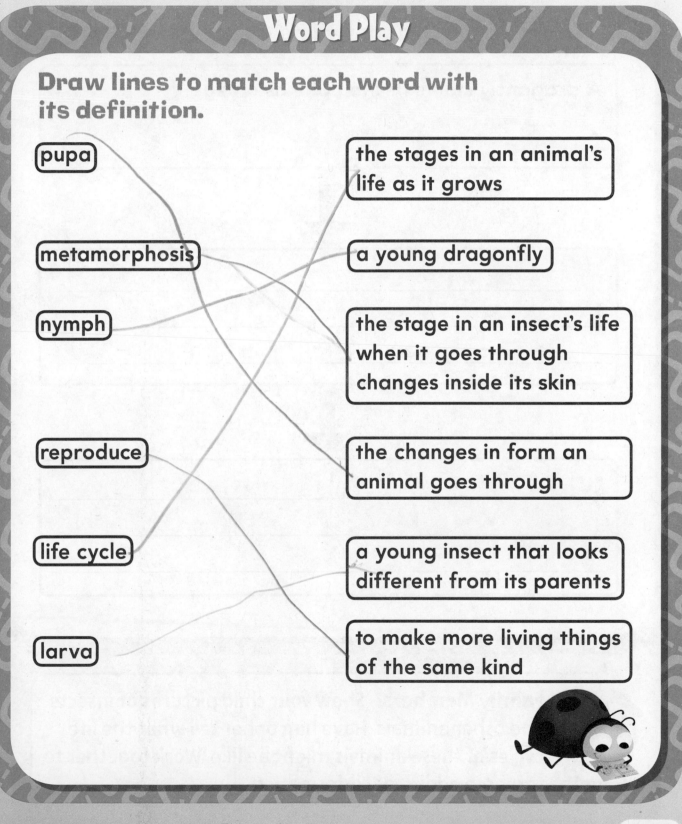

pupa — the stages in an animal's life as it grows

metamorphosis — a young dragonfly

nymph — the stage in an insect's life when it goes through changes inside its skin

reproduce — the changes in form an animal goes through

life cycle — a young insect that looks different from its parents

larva — to make more living things of the same kind

Fill in the chart. Name and explain the stages that dragonflies go through during their life cycle.

Dragonfly Life Cycle

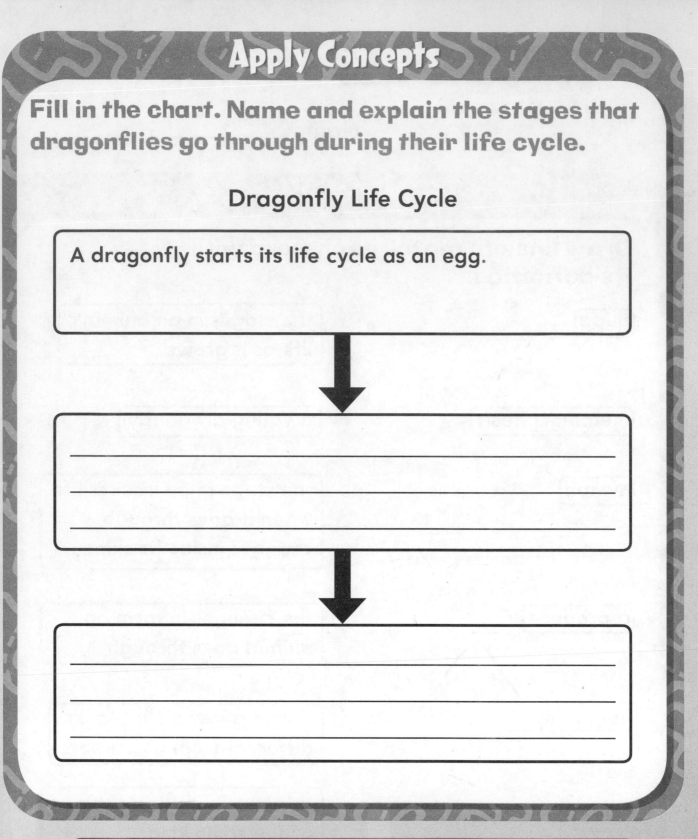

A dragonfly starts its life cycle as an egg.

Take It Home!

Family Members: Show your child pictures of insects and other animals. Have him or her tell what the life cycles of these animals might be like. Work together to research additional information.

394

TEKS 2.10B observe, record, and compare how the physical characteristics of plants help them meet their basic needs such as stems carry water throughout the plant

Lesson **4**

Essential Question

What Are Some Plant Parts?

Engage Your Brain!

Find the answer to the question in the lesson.

This flower smells bad to attract insects.

Why do flowers attract insects?

_____

Active Reading

Lesson Vocabulary

❶ Preview the lesson.

❷ Write the 3 vocabulary terms here.

_____   _____

_____

A Part to Play

Plants need sunlight, air, water, and nutrients from the soil to grow. Each part of a plant helps the plant get what it needs to live and grow.

Flowers, leaves, stems, and roots are important parts of a plant. Find these parts in the picture.

▶ Circle the stem.
Mark an X on the flower.
Draw a box around a leaf.

flower

leaf

stem

roots

Do the Job

Flowers help plants make new plants. Parts of a flower make seeds that grow into new plants.

_____

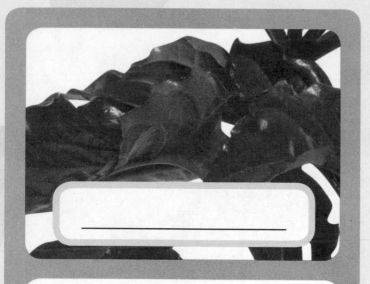

_____

Leaves make food for the plant. They use air, water, and sunlight to make the food.

▶ Write a label on each line to name the plant part in the picture.

_____

Stems carry water and nutrients from the roots to the leaves and other parts of the plant. They also hold up the plant.

_____

The roots grow into the soil and hold the plant in place. They take in water and nutrients from the soil.

Flower Power

The plant part that makes seeds is the flower. The flower has its own parts, too. Some parts of a flower are pollen, petals, and seeds.

Active Reading

A detail is a fact about a main idea. Draw one line under a detail. Draw an arrow to the main idea it tells about.

Flowers make pollen. **Pollen** is a powder that flowers need to make seeds. Most plants use pollen from other flowers to make seeds. Insects, animals, and wind may carry pollen from one flower to another.

The colorful petals attract insects and animals. A plant may need insects and animals to move pollen.

Flowers make seeds. A new plant may grow from a **seed**.

▶ What part of a plant grows into a new plant?

_____

Sum It Up!

1 Label It!

Label the parts of the plant.

_____

_____

2 Match It!

Match the plant part to what it does.

hold plant in place

carry water from the roots

makes food

Name _____

Word Play

Read the clues. Use the words to complete the puzzle.

| leaf | stem | flower | seed | roots | pollen |

Across

1. plant part that makes food

2. take in water from the soil

3. carries water from the roots

Down

4. powder that helps make seeds

5. plant part with petals

6. grows into new plants

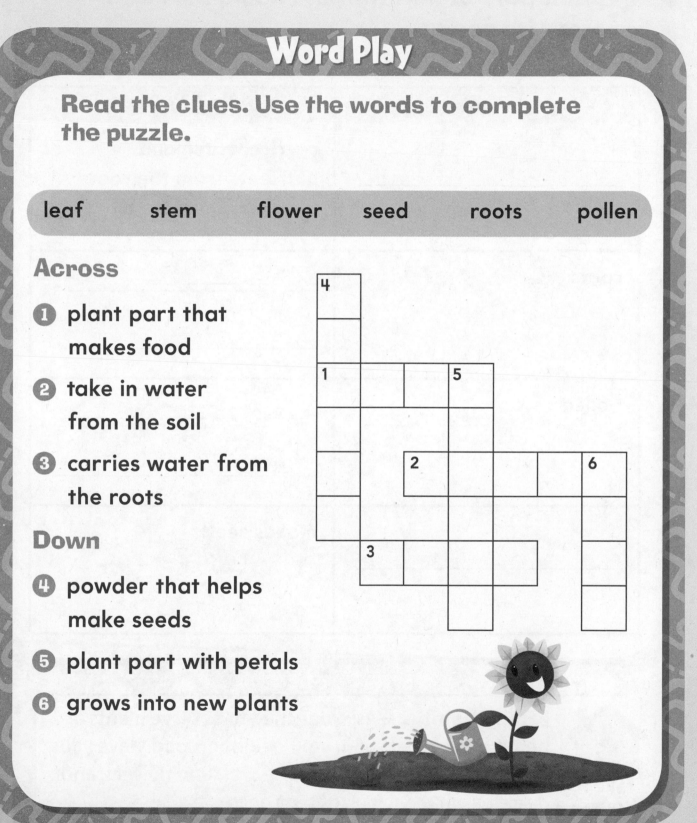

Apply Concepts

Fill in the chart. Record the name of the plant part or how the part helps the plant meet its needs.

Plant Parts

Part	What It Does
_____	carries water and nutrients from the roots to other plant parts
roots	_____ _____
pollen	_____ _____
_____	makes seeds

Take It Home!

Family Members: Ask your child to observe plants at home, in a garden, or in your neighborhood. Have your child identify the roots, stem, leaves, and flowers, and describe what each plant part does.

Get to Know...

Dr. Maria Elena Zavala

As a young girl, Maria Elena Zavala thought a lot about plants. Her grandmother lived next door. She grew plants to use as medicine. Young Maria learned about those plants from her grandmother.

Today Maria Elena Zavala is a botanist and a teacher. A botanist is a scientist who studies plants. Dr. Zavala studies how plants respond to their environment. She and her students are finding out how roots grow.

Fun Fact

As a child, Maria took apart her father's roses to learn more about plants.

405

Now You Be a Botanist!

▶ Explore what botanists do. Draw and label roots, flowers, and leaves on this plant.

TEKS **2.10B** observe, record, and compare how the physical characteristics of plants help them meet their basic needs such as stems carry water throughout the plant

Lesson **5**

Essential Question

What Are Some Plant Life Cycles?

Engage Your Brain!

Find the answer to the question in this lesson.

What does the flower part of a dandelion make?

It makes _____.

Active Reading

Lesson Vocabulary

1. Preview the lesson.

2. Write the 4 vocabulary terms here.

_____   _____

_____   _____

Plant Start-Ups

Plants are living things. They grow and change. They have life cycles. Most plant life cycles begin with a **seed**. New plants grow from seeds. The growing plants start to look like their parent plants.

Active Reading

Find the words that tell about seeds. Draw a line under the words.

The plants in this garden grew from seeds.

How Fast Do Plants Grow?

Some plants grow quickly. Plants in a vegetable garden take just a few months to become adult plants. Other plants, such as trees, take many years to become adults.

Do the Math!
Interpret a Table

Use the chart to answer the question.

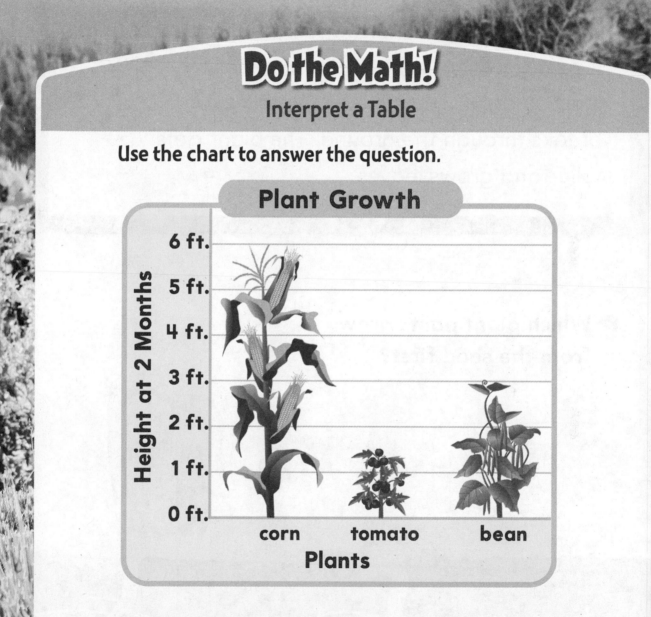

Plant Growth

Height at 2 Months: 6 ft., 5 ft., 4 ft., 3 ft., 2 ft., 1 ft., 0 ft.

Plants: corn, tomato, bean

▶ How much taller did the corn plant grow than the bean plant?

Start with a Seed

What happens when you plant a seed? When a seed gets warmth, air, and water, it may germinate. **Germinate** means to start to grow. The stem of the tiny plant breaks through the ground. The plant gets taller and grows leaves.

▶ Which plant parts grow from the seed first?

_____

A tiny plant is inside a seed.

The seed germinates. The roots grow down.

The stem grows up toward the light.

Growing Up

The tiny plant inside the seed has become a young plant called a **seedling**.

The seedling grows into an adult plant. An adult plant can make flowers and seeds.

Active Reading

Find the words that tell the meaning of **seedling**. Draw a line under those words.

The plant grows more roots and leaves.

The adult plant grows flowers.

Apples
All Around

Some plants have flowers that make seeds and fruit. Parts of the flower grow into fruit. The fruit grows around the seeds to hold and protect them.

Active Reading

Circle the word **seeds** each time you see it on these two pages.

apple blossoms

Parts of apple blossoms grow into apples. The apples grow around seeds.

A Long Life

Some plants have short lives. They die soon after their flowers make seeds. Other plants, such as apple trees, can live for many years. An apple tree can live for a hundred years or more!

adult apple tree

▶ **What do apple blossoms make?**

_____

Inside a Cone

Some plants, like pine trees, do not have flowers. But they do have seeds. Where do their seeds grow? A **cone** is a part of a pine tree and some other plants. Seeds grow inside the cone.

closed pinecones

open pinecones with seeds

The cone protects the seeds until they are ready to germinate. Then the cone opens up, and the seeds can fall out.

▶ Where do pine seeds form?

Pine Tree Beginnings

Pine seeds fall to the ground and germinate. As the seedlings grow, they start to look like their parent plants. After a few years, the pine trees grow cones and make seeds. The life cycle begins again.

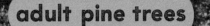

adult pine trees

▶ What happens after an adult pine tree grows cones and makes seeds?

_____

_____

Sum It Up!

① Draw It!

Draw the missing step in the plant's life cycle. Label your picture.

seed

_____

seedling

adult

② Mark It!

Draw an X on the plant part that does not have seeds.

③ Think About It!

How are flowers and pinecones alike?

_____

_____

Name _____

Word Play

Read each word. Trace a path through the maze to connect each word to its picture.

| seed | cone | flower | seedling |

Apply Concepts

Write to tell about the life cycle of a plant. Use the words <u>germinate</u>, <u>seed</u>, and <u>seedling</u>.

Life Cycle of a Plant

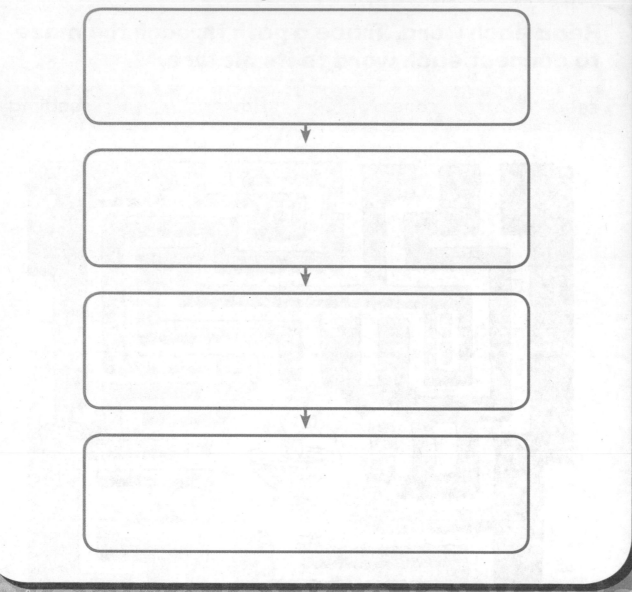

Family Members: Ask your child to tell you about plant life cycles. Then take a walk around your neighborhood. Talk about the plants you see.

Take It Home!

Name _____

Essential Question

How Does a Bean Plant Grow?

TEKS **2.2A** ask questions about organisms, objects, and events during observations and investigations **2.2B** plan and conduct descriptive investigations such as how organisms grow **2.2D** record and organize data using pictures, numbers, and words **2.2E** communicate observations and justify explanations using student-generated data from simple descriptive investigations **2.4B** measure and compare organisms and objects using non-standard units that that approximate metric units **2.10B** observe, record, and compare how the physical characteristics of plants help them meet their basic needs such as stems carry water throughout the plant

Set a Purpose

Explain what you will learn from this activity.

_____

_____

Think About the Procedure

1 Why must you give the plant water and sunlight?

_____

_____

2 Compare the way that your bean plant grew with the way that a classmate's bean plant grew. What was the same?

_____

_____

_____

Record Your Data

Record what you observe. Measure your bean plant using both standard and non-standard units. Compare your plant's measurements with those of a classmate.

Date	Observations

Draw Conclusions

How did the bean plant change?

_____

_____

_____

Ask More Questions

What other questions could you ask about how plants grow?

_____

_____

TEKS 2.3A identify and explain a problem in his/her own words and propose a task and solution for the problem such as lack of water in a habitat

S.T.E.M.
Engineering and Technology

Bringing Water to Plants

Drip Irrigation

Irrigation is a way to get water to land so plants can grow. A lawn sprinkler is one kind of irrigation.

Drip irrigation is another kind of irrigation. Hoses carry water to plants. Water drips from emitters on the hoses. This brings water right to the soil around the plants. Less water is wasted. Less water evaporates.

emitter

hose

Two Ways

Compare sprinkler irrigation and drip irrigation. Write a possible good thing and bad thing about each system.

Good _____   Good _____

_____   _____

Bad _____   Bad _____

_____   _____

Build On It!

Compare different kinds of drip irrigation. Complete **Compare It: Drip Tips** on the Inquiry Flipchart.

Vocabulary Review

Use the terms in the box to complete the sentences.

insect
metamorphosis
pollen

TEKS 2.10B

1. The powder that flowers need to make seeds is _____.

TEKS 2.10C

2. Changes some animals go through are called _____.

TEKS 2.10A

3. A(n) _____ has three body parts and a hard outer covering.

Science Concepts

Fill in the letter of the choice that best answers the question.

TEKS 2.10A

4. How do fins help fish?

Ⓐ Fins help fish balance and steer.

Ⓑ Fins help fish take in oxygen.

Ⓒ Fins help fish lay eggs.

TEKS 2.10B

5. Compare roots and stems. How are they alike?

Ⓐ They hold up a plant.

Ⓑ They can move nutrients.

Ⓒ They keep a plant in soil.

TEKS 2.10C

6. Look at these stages of a butterfly life cycle.

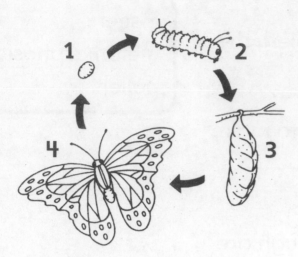

What do you think is happening in Step 2?

Ⓐ An adult lays eggs.

Ⓑ A larva hatches and grows fast.

Ⓒ A larva becomes a pupa.

TEKS 2.10C

7. What is a unique life cycle step insects go through that mammals do not?

Ⓐ adult

Ⓑ larva

Ⓒ young

TEKS 2.10A

8. What group of animals has fur or hair to keep them warm?

Ⓐ amphibians

Ⓑ mammals

Ⓒ reptiles

9. How are the life cycles of an apple tree and a pine tree the same?

Ⓐ They both have flowers that grow into fruits.

Ⓑ They both have cones that hold seeds.

Ⓒ They both make seeds.

TEKS 2.10B

10. What does this plant part do?

A) It makes food.

B) It grows into a new plant.

C) It carries water to other parts of the plant.

TEKS 2.10A

11. Which animal groups lay their eggs in water?

A) amphibians and fish

B) fish and reptiles

C) birds and fish

TEKS 2.10C

12. What can an adult insect do that a larva cannot?

A) eat

B) grow

C) reproduce

TEKS 2.10B

13. Identify the plant part shown here.

How does it help the plant meet its basic needs?

A) It grows into fruit, which covers the seeds.

B) It makes food from air, water, and sunlight.

C) It makes seeds, which grow into new plants.

Inquiry and the Big Idea

Write the answers to these questions.

TEKS 2.10B

14. Look at this plant.

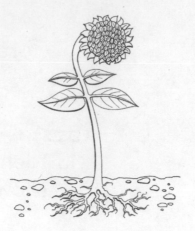

How does water move through the plant? How is water used in the different parts of the plant?

_____

_____

TEKS 2.10A

15. Look at this animal. Name two parts that help the animal meet its needs. Describe how the parts help the animal meet its needs.

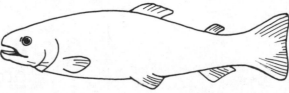

_____

_____

_____

Interactive Glossary

This Interactive Glossary will help you learn how to spell a vocabulary term. The Glossary will give you the meaning of the term. It will also show you a picture to help you understand what the term means.

Where you see **Your Turn** write your own words or draw your own picture to help you remember what the term means.

Glossary Pronunciation Key

With every glossary term, there is also a phonetic respelling. A phonetic respelling writes the word the way it sounds, which can help you pronounce new or unfamiliar words. Use this key to help you understand the respellings.

Sound	As in	Phonetic Respelling	Sound	As in	Phonetic Respelling
a	bat	(BAT)	oh	over	(OH·ver)
ah	lock	(LAHK)	oo	pool	(POOL)
air	rare	(RAIR)	ow	out	(OWT)
ar	argue	(AR·gyoo)	oy	foil	(FOYL)
aw	law	(LAW)	s	cell	(SEL)
ay	face	(FAYS)		sit	(SIT)
ch	chapel	(CHAP·uhl)	sh	sheep	(SHEEP)
e	test	(TEST)	th	that	(THAT)
	metric	(MEH·trik)		thin	(THIN)
ee	eat	(EET)	u	pull	(PUL)
	feet	(FEET)	uh	medal	(MED·uhl)
	ski	(SKEE)		talent	(TAL·uhnt)
er	paper	(PAY·per)		pencil	(PEN·suhl)
	fern	(FERN)		onion	(UHN·yuhn)
eye	idea	(eye·DEE·uh)		playful	(PLAY·fuhl)
i	bit	(BIT)		dull	(DUHL)
ing	going	(GOH·ing)	y	yes	(YES)
k	card	(KARD)		ripe	(RYP)
	kite	(KYT)	z	bags	(BAGZ)
ngk	bank	(BANGK)	zh	treasure	(TREZH·er)

Interactive Glossary

A

adaptation (ad·uhp·TAY·shuhn)
Something that helps a living thing survive in its environment. (p. 346)

amphibian (am·FIB·ee·uhn)
The group of animals with smooth, wet skin. Young amphibians live in the water, and most adults live on land. (p. 375)

attract (uh·TRAKT)
To pull toward something. (p. 149)

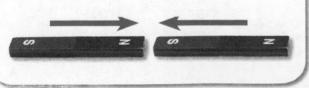

B

basic needs (BAY·sik NEEDZ)
Certain things, such as food, water, air, and shelter, that a living thing needs to live and grow. (p. 302)

bird (BURD)
The group of animals with feathers on their bodies and wings. Most birds can fly. (p. 373)

Your Turn

C

communicate
(kuh·MYOO·ni·kayt)

To write, draw, or speak to show what you have learned. (p. 31)

condense (kuh·DENS)

To change from a gas into tiny drops of water. (p. 239)

cone (KOHN)

A part of a pine tree and some other plants where seeds form. (p. 414)

conserve (kuhn·SERV)

To use things wisely to make them last longer. (p. 208)

constellation
(kahn·stuh·LAY·shuhn)

A group of stars that seems to form a pattern. (p. 273)

Interactive Glossary

D

design process
(dih·ZYN PRAHS·es)
A set of steps that engineers follow to solve problems. (p. 47)

dispose (dis·POZ)
To get rid of something. (p. 212)

Your Turn

dormancy (DAWR·muhn·see)
A time when plants stop growing. (p. 251)

draw conclusions
(DRAW kuhn·KLOO·zhuhnz)
To use information gathered during an investigation to see whether the results support the hypothesis. (p. 31)

energy (EN·er·jee)

Something that can cause matter to move or change. (p. 120)

engineer (en·juh·NEER)

A person who uses math and science to design technology that solves problems. (p. 46)

environment (en·VY·ruhn·mehnt)

All the living and nonliving things in a place. (pp. 66, 332)

evaporate (ee·VAP·uh·rayt)

To change from a liquid into a gas. (p. 238)

Your Turn

Interactive Glossary

evaporation
(ee·vap·uh·RAY·shuhn)
The process by which liquid water changes into water vapor, a gas. (p. 101)

flower (FLOW·er)
The plant part that helps a plant make new plants. Part of the flower makes seeds that grow into new plants. (p. 398)

F

fish (FISH)
The group of animals that live in water and get oxygen through gills. Fish have scales and use fins to swim and balance. (p. 376)

food chain
(FOOD CHAYN)
A path that shows how energy moves from plants to animals. (p. 338)

Your Turn

G

force (FAWRS)
A push or a pull that makes an object move or stop moving. (p. 136)

gas (GAS)
A state of matter that fills all the space of its container. (p. 89)

Your Turn

fresh water (FRESH WAW·ter)
Water that has very little salt in it. (p. 182)

germinate (JER·mi·nayt)
To start to grow. (p. 410)

Interactive Glossary

gills (GILZ)
The parts of some animals that take in oxygen from the water. (p. 305)

heat (HEET)
A kind of energy that makes things warmer. (p. 121)

glacier (GLAY·sher)
A large, thick sheet of slow-moving ice. (p. 182)

Your Turn

hibernate (HY·ber·nayt)
To go into a deep, sleeplike state for winter. (p. 251)

human-made resource
(HYOO·**muhn**-MAYD REE·**sawrs**)

Anything made by humans
for people to use.
Human-made resources
cannot be found in nature.
(p. 194)

inquiry skills
(IN·**kwer**·ee SKILZ)

The skills people use to find
out information. (p. 4)

hypothesis (hy·PAWTH·uh·sis)

A statement that you can
test. (p. 29)

insect (IN·**sekt**)

A kind of animal that has
three body parts and six
legs. (p. 377)

Interactive Glossary

investigate (in·VES·tuh·gayt)
To plan and do a test to answer a question or solve a problem. (p. 28)

life cycle (LYF SY·kuhl)
Changes that happen to an animal or a plant during its life. (p. 386)

L

larva (LAR·vuh)
A young insect that looks different from its parents. (p. 388)

Your Turn

light (LYT)
A kind of energy that lets you see. (p. 121)

loudness (LOWD·nuhs)
How loud or soft a sound is. (p. 127)

lungs (LUHNGZ)
The parts of humans and some animals that help them breathe by taking in oxygen from the air. (p. 304)

liquid (LIK·wid)
A state of matter that takes the shape of its container. (p. 88)

Your Turn

Interactive Glossary

M

magnet (MAG·nit)
An object that can pull things made of iron or steel and can push or pull other magnets. (p. 148)

mammal (MAM·uhl)
The group of animals with hair or fur on their bodies. (p. 372)

mass (MAS)
The amount of matter in an object. (p. 82)

matter (MAT·er)
Anything that takes up space and has mass. (p. 82)

Your Turn

metamorphosis (met·uh·MAWR·fuh·sis)
A series of changes in appearance that some animals go through. (p. 388)

migrate (MY·grayt)
To travel from one place to another and back again. (p. 251)

Your Turn

natural resource (NACH·er·uhl REE·sawrs)
Anything from nature that people can use. (p. 190)

nutrients (NOO·tree·uhnts)
Substances that help plants grow. (p. 317)

motion (MOH·shuhn)
When something is moving. Things are in motion when they move. (p. 136)

Interactive Glossary

nymph (NIMF)

A young insect that looks a lot like its parents. (p. 390)

phases (FAYZ·ez)

The shapes of the moon you see as it moves. (p. 286)

orbit (AWR·bit)

The path a planet takes as it moves around the sun. Earth's orbit around the sun takes one year. (p. 270)

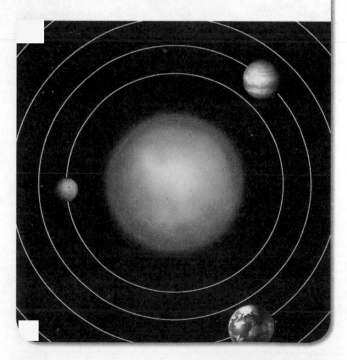

pitch (PICH)

How high or low a sound is. (p. 126)

planet (PLAN·it)

A large ball of rock or gas that moves around the sun. Earth is our planet. (p. 268)

pollen (PAWL·uhn)

A powder that flowers need to make seeds. Some small animals help carry pollen from one flower to another. (pp. 337, 400)

pole (POHL)

A place on a magnet where the pull is the greatest. (p. 148)

Your Turn

precipitation
(pri·sip·uh·TAY·shuhn)

Water that falls from the sky. Rain, snow, sleet, and hail are kinds of precipitation. (p. 228)

Interactive Glossary

property (PRAH·per·tee)
One part of what something is like. Color, shape, size, and texture are each a property. (p. 83)

pupa (PYOO·puh)
The part of a life cycle when an insect makes a hard outer covering. (p. 389)

R

recycle (ree·sy·kuhl)
To use the materials in old things to make new things. (p. 211)

Your Turn

reduce (ree·DOOS)
To use less of something.
(p. 211)

reproduce (ree·pruh·DOOS)
To have young, or more living things, of the same kind.
(p. 384)

reptile (REP·tyl)
The group of animals with dry skin covered in scales.
(p. 374)

repel (rih·PEL)
To push away from something. (p. 149)

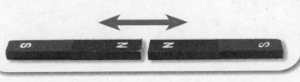

Interactive Glossary

reuse (ree·YOOZ)
To use something again.
(p. 210)

rotate (ROH·tayt)
To turn. Day and night
happen when Earth rotates.
(p. 280)

rock (RAHK)
A hard, non-living object
from the ground. (p.168)

Your Turn

S

salt water (SAWLT WAW·ter)
Water that has a large
amount of salt in it. (p. 184)

science tools (SY·uhns TOOLZ)
The tools people use to find out information. (p. 16)

Your Turn

seed (SEED)
The part of a plant that new plants may grow from. (pp. 401, 408)

season (SEE·zuhn)
A time of year that has a certain kind of weather. The four seasons are spring, summer, fall, and winter. (p. 248)

seedling (SEED·ling)
A young plant. (p. 411)

Interactive Glossary

shelter (SHEL·ter)
A safe place to live. (p. 307)

solar system
(SOH·ler SIS·tuhm)
The sun, the planets, and the planets' moons that move around the sun. (p. 268)

solid (SAHL·id)
The only state of matter that has its own shape. (p. 87)

sound (SOWND)
Energy you can hear. (p. 120)

speed (SPEED)

The measure of an object's change in position during a certain amount of time. (p. 138)

survive (ser·VYV)

To stay alive. (p. 302)

star (STAR)

A large ball of hot gases that gives off light and heat. The sun is the closest star to Earth. (p. 272)

Your Turn

Interactive Glossary

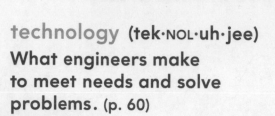

technology (tek·NOL·uh·jee)
What engineers make to meet needs and solve problems. (p. 60)

temperature
(TEM·per·uh·cher)
A measure of how hot or cold something is. You can measure temperature with a thermometer. (p. 228)

thermometer
(ther·MAHM·uh·ter)
A tool used to measure temperature. (p. 17)

Your Turn

V

vibrate (VY·brayt)

To move back and forth very quickly. (p. 126)

volume (VAHL·yoom)

The amount of space that matter takes up. (p. 88)

Your Turn

W

water cycle (WAW·ter SY·kuhl)

The movement of water from Earth to the air and back again. (p. 238)

water vapor (WAW·ter VAY·per)

Water in the form of a gas. (p. 101)

weather (WEH·ther)

What the air outside is like. (p. 224)

Interactive Glossary

weather pattern
(WEH·ther PAT·ern)
A weather change that repeats over and over.
(p. 236)

Your Turn

weathering (WEH·ther·ing)
A kind of change that happens when wind and water break down rock into smaller pieces. (p. 169)

wind (WIND)
Moving air that surrounds us and takes up space. (p. 228)

Index

Index

Index

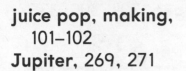

Index

Index

Index